for the
Love of Roses
in florida and elsewhere

Barbara Oehlbeck

Great Outdoors Publishing Co.
St. Petersburg, Florida

117336

Copyright © 2000 Barbara Oehlbeck.
All Rights Reserved.
First Edition.

International Standard Book Number 0-8200-0419-7
Library of Congress Card Number 00-109200

Published by: Great Outdoors Publishing Co.
4747 28th Street North
St. Petersburg, Florida 33714
(727)525-6609

Publisher's Cataloging in Publication Data
(Provided by Quality Books, Inc.)

Oehlbeck, Barbara.
    For the love of roses in Florida and elsewhere /
Barbara Oehlbeck. -- 1st ed.
    p. cm.
    Includes bibliographical references and index.
    LCCN: 00-109200
    ISBN: 0-8200-0419-7

    1. Roses--Florida. 2. Rose culture--Florida.
I. Title.

SB411.O34 2000   635.9'33734'09759
                        QBI00-840

Cover: Counter-clockwise from top are 'Milestone,'
'Mr. Lincoln,' 'Brandy,' 'Pure Poetry,' and
'Hannah Gordon.'

Printed in the United States of America

Permissions:
    The essays "Grafted vs. Own-Root Roses" and "Ultimate
        Easy Roses," and Appendix B, "Roses that Can Be
        Grown in Central Florida without Spraying," all by
        Dr. Malcolm Manners, are reprinted from *The Cherokee
        Rose,* newsletter of the Central Florida Heritage Rose
        Society, and are used with permission.
    "Miniatures: The World of Marvelous Little Roses," by
        Sean McCann, is used with permission.
    "David Austin Roses You Can Live With," by Jim Small, is
        reprinted from *Wind Chimes,* newsletter of the Central
        Florida Rose Society, and is used with permission.
    "Growing 'Show' Roses," by Doug Whitt, is used with per-
        mission.
    "New Developments in Organic Gardening," by Gene
        McAvoy, UF/IFAS Extension Agent, Hendry County, is
        used with permission.
    "ARS Consulting Rosarians—A Valuable Resource," by
        Steve Jones, is used with permission.
    "The Rose is the Key that Unlocks the Memories," by
        Tricia Pursley, is used with permission.
    "A Rose by Any Other Name..." by Dr. Derek Burch, is
        used with permission.
    "I Know Who to Call," by Diana Richards, is used with
        permission.

Photos:
    Photo on page 20 by Roger Kilgore, courtesy Nelsons'
        Florida Roses, Apopka, FL.
    Photos on page 23 ('Green Rose'), page 24 ('Sun Flare'),
        page 25 ('Brigadoon') and page 52 ('Hannah Gordon')
        by C. C. F. Gachet.
    Photo on page 27 ("Peace, Oh Perfect Peace") by
        Barbara Oehlbeck.
    Photo of Dolly Parton on page 33 courtesy of Dolly Parton
        Productions, Pigeon Forge, TN.
    Photos on pages 35, 36 and 38 courtesy of Sean McCann.
    Photo on page 79 courtesy of Wayside Gardens, Hodges, SC.
    Front cover photos of 'Hannah Gordon' and 'Brandy' by
        Dr. Luther Oehlbeck; 'Milestone,' 'Mr. Lincoln' and
        'Pure Poetry' by Jan Allyn.
    Back cover photo of 'Diana' courtesy Bear Creek Gardens,
        Jackson & Perkins Roses, Somis, CA.
    All other photos are from The Captain's Collection, by
        Dr. Luther W. Oehlbeck.

For the Captain, again and always…

The greatest gifts:

You, morning, and roses…

I am born again.

CONTENTS

ACKNOWLEDGMENTS
To My Beloved Friends in the Garden

This book is filled with the love of roses from many as deeply devoted to them as I am. The extraordinary contribution of each who has given time and knowledge to this work is like the joy of adding another rose to the garden.

All of you, individually and collectively, have made this project an experience I can only liken to the love and beauty of actually growing roses.

My deepest gratitude is extended to:

The Captain, whose patience with my passion for roses is surpassed only by his most-of-the-time patience for my projects, various and sundry. Without his magnificent willingness to read, edit, critique, laugh or cry, I'd have to give up.

Jan Allyn, editor/publisher, who "weeded the garden" with grace and tact through the rose garden pages, exhibiting one and all to best advantage. Hers was the magic wand that brought all the loves happily together. ✸ Theresa Artuso, president Burner & Co., who highly recommends roses in her landscape designs. ✸ Mel Bough, who shares all he grows and knows with grace and generosity. ✸ Betty Dickey, who gives to all within reach. ✸ Diane and Jim Giles, who sell their "Florida" roses but "give" their love for them. ✸ The late Dr. Margaret Pfluge Gregory, who exhibited the epitome of grace and generosity in aiding me in all sorts of botanical matters, with love and devotion. No hour was too early or too late. In editing the manuscript, with incredible plant knowledge, she and her husband, the late Dr. Walton Gregory, ploughed through potential inaccuracies until they were not only botanically correct but so that, like Dr. Derek Burch said, "the voice in the garden" was not lost. ✸ Bob Grant, who expounds on fragrance in roses. ✸ Dot Jackson, who gives from her wealth of knowledge about writing and editing, and the heart of "her mountains" of which she is an integral part. ✸ Steve Jones, National Consulting Rosarian and Chairman, who "wrote the book" on Consulting Rosarians. ✸ Dr. Malcolm Manners, authority on Old Garden and old English roses. ✸ Gene McAvoy, Hendry County Extension Agent, who's elevated the art of Florida gardening. ✸ Sean McCann, who has the incredible ability to inspire people and projects, even from half a world away, and whose immense talent is surpassed only by his marvelous spirit. ✸ Tim Myer, Orban's Nursery, who's added much to 'Fortuniana' rootstock rose gardens. ✸ Mark Nelson, whose Nelsons' Florida Roses are to gardens what oranges are to Florida groves. ✸ Dolly Parton and her agent, Ted Williams, who graciously permitted use of her extraordinary photo. Her rose typifies the lady herself! ✸ Tricia Pursley, whose sparkling spirit, incredible ideas, wealth of knowledge, and abilities are constant inspiration, in the garden and out. Wonder what it would feel like to be an inspiration to a rose… ✸ Diana Richards, who sculpts porcelain roses more lifelike than some in her garden! ✸ Eula and Carroll Richards, whose rose-growing ability is exceeded only by their untiring teaching skills to individuals and groups. ✸ Jim Scrivner, who's proven his love for roses and those who grow them, one bush or a hundred. In an era when most independent garden centers have died and gone to Heaven, Jim has kept the faith on Earth, not only in growing roses but in the joy of gardening itself. ✸ Isabelle de Sercey, who demonstrates common-sense rose growing in North Florida. ✸ Bill and Mary Maude Sharpe, who give to all within sight of their gardens. ✸ Jim Small, whose love is David Austin roses. ✸ Perry Sneed, administrative director of marketing (retired), Bearcreek Gardens/Jackson & Perkins, who listened and advised with gifted understanding and encouragemen, and led me to Dr. Keith Zary, who graciously offered expert advice and support. ✸ Howard Walters, whose "Rosarian Ramblings" advice is pure gold in the garden. ✸ Doug Whitt, for his in-depth piece on "show" roses. ✸ Lynn and Rusty Woods, whose roses are surpassed only by their joy in giving them away. ✸ Richard Workman, president Coastplan, Fort Myers, Florida, who's always gone that extra mile for my efforts.

And last, though certainly not least, my grandfather Glenn F. Harding, who spent most of his life as a wood carver/designer. Yet, his first love was for the land and everything that came from it, not the least of which were the roses he grew for my grandmother in a small plot by the kitchen window.

The sweetest rose to me, is the rose I see with Thee.

TRIBUTES

Just as there is truly no way at times to describe an exquisite rose, there is no way at times to express adequate appreciation and gratitude. This is one of those times.

Dr. Derek Burch "walked" into our rose garden and immediately understood and appreciated, both professionally and personally, the task at hand: a manuscript about growing roses in Florida and elsewhere. Fact is, we are still looking forward to meeting him in person, to give him an armful of roses and untold gratitude for his taking *For the Love of Roses* under his wing, reorganizing the material, making botanical corrections, and generally polishing, polishing, always respecting—in his words—"the voice in the garden."

Dr. Burch holds far more than a Ph.D. in systematic botany/statistics from the University of Florida, Master of Science degree in plant pathology and also in agricultural botany from the University of Wales; he holds the highest degree in thoughtfulness and consideration for the heart of this work. He's been a nursery owner, teacher, extension specialist, horticulturist/administrator in botanical gardens, including the Missouri Botanical Gardens, Montreal Botanical Gardens and the esteemed Fairchild Tropical Gardens in Miami. He is an accomplished writer and editor and the list goes on and on, through many gardens reaching all the way to his native England. Without his expertise and incredible knowledge in these many fields, this book would not have become a reality. We are deeply thankful to have had his extraordinary mastery reflecting his genuine love of plants in our "garden" which has become *For the Love of Roses*.

His horticultural excellence also includes his current role as editor-in-chief of an on-line publication at Betrock Information Systems website, www.hortworld.com.

Dr. Keith W. Zary, vice president of research at Bearcreek Gardens/Jackson & Perkins Roses, has more stars in his crown of accomplishments in the world of roses than can be carried around easily! He has sole responsibility for some 400,000 varieties, from which 2,000 to 3,000 are propagated and stringently evaluated for everything from disease resistance to bloom profusion. And yet, in some way amongst all these roses, his own love of roses inspired him to find enough time and enthusiasm to review this book!

How do you express proper appreciation for such a gift?

Among Dr. Zary's most recent triumphs is his creation of the rose honoring the memory of Diana, Princess of Wales, described as an ivory-colored rose with a pink blush, now available on 'Fortuniana' rootstock, as well as 'Dr. Huey' through Jackson & Perkins catalog.

Also, Dr. Zary has recently won major European awards in England, the Netherlands and Germany, including the President's International Trophy of the Royal National Rose Society. He is only the second breeder from the United States to ever win this prestigious English award. He is also the first U.S. breeder since 1955 to take home the coveted Golden Rose of the Hague (Netherlands), an honor made all the more significant by the fact that it is bestowed on a commercial breeder by his peers, a group of experts from around the entire world.

Other outstanding awards include two out of four AARS winners for 1998, 'Opening Night'/HT and 'Fame!'/Grandiflora. Dr. Zary's 'Candelabra'/Grandiflora won the AARS award in 1999, and his 2000 award winner is 'Gemini'/HT.

A shy, soft-spoken, unassuming scientist who has worked for more than a decade in the well-tended obscurity of an unmarked rose research facility in the rolling hills of Somis, California, Dr. Zary lives in nearby Thousand Oaks.

The wondrous splendor of living with and loving roses.

INTRODUCTION

Shhh… The rose is speaking.

As is the case with most things, no one book or person, no one set of instructions, no one class or series of studies will tell you everything you need or want to know about growing roses. In fact, after all is said and done in the garden, it just may be that growing roses is more of an art than a science. However, those who have contributed to this book believe that the information in its pages will "open the garden gate" for you to enjoy the rewards of growing roses. If you don't find exactly the answer you're looking for here, we have provided a list of resources from which further information can be obtained.

The first part of this book is about the roses themselves. To the new grower, the choices to be made re rootstock, growth habit and variety, et cetera can be dizzying, and the color choices dazzling. Selecting plants that do what you want them to do and that will thrive in your plot of ground is the first step—but perhaps the most important one—toward a successful rose garden.

Part two details the activities that make the "art" of growing roses—in Florida or elsewhere—a thoroughly happy and satisfying experience. These include selecting healthy plants, choosing a suitable location, using proper soil, applying water and fertilizer, pruning, and controlling pests and diseases.

Part three is about the manifold blessings, the inspiring beauty and pure joy that roses give in the garden, in the home, and to friends. To some the satisfaction in growing roses is determined by the size of blooms and their absolute perfection, a totally worthwhile goal deserving of admiration. However, to us there is a unique charm in those roses that are small, or at times even misshapen—roses that would never get through a rose show door, let alone make it to the show table. But oh, the endearing smiles and expressions of affection they bring to those whose lives don't ordinarily include roses. When being accused of being prejudiced, we simply admit to being guilty as charged. After all, like my grandfather, we could never admit to looking upon an ugly rose.

In part four, various growers from here and yon lend their voices, sharing their expertise, personal experiences, "portraits" of their own rose-growing efforts, funny scenarios and flights of fancy.

Part five is a rose potpourri, in which a few who truly love roses tell their varied tales about their own or others' roses—which brings us to the happy conclusion that after all is said and done, the roses are planted, they grow and bloom and their joy and fragrance is all about. And we, their dedicated caretakers and guardians, are enchanted with their gifts to us, some perfect, some not so perfect, but all cherished as the fruit of our love, our labors and pure devotion.

After all, perhaps this is what the love of roses really is.

Firstlight.
All is silent in the garden…
Until one rose sings to another, and another…
Then suddenly, all together, one glorious ode to joy!

1. Choosing Roses for Your Garden

HELP! HOW SHALL I CHOOSE WHICH ROSE TO PLANT?

This question raises others that have remarkably rewarding answers. Which roses please you most esthetically: color, form, shape of bush, et cetera? Considering these same factors, which roses will fit into your landscape plan? Do you like a manicured look, or do you prefer a more natural, casual appearance? How much time and effort are you willing to put into the care of your roses? Is fragrance an important consideration? Are you perhaps leaning toward a "potted" rose garden, on a sunny deck or patio, apron of a pool, or even hanging from the eaves?

Naturally, there are all sorts of variations on the answers to these questions. Before examining them in detail, it should be pointed out that if you desire a garden in a mostly-shaded area, you would be wise to choose another plant entirely because roses are purely sun-loving. They will not be happy in less than five to six hours of full sun daily, and they prefer morning sun. They need strong sunlight, too—not come-and-go rays slanting through the leaves of trees. Though some rose varieties perform better in less sun than others, even they will not thrive and bloom in a location that is shady. Seldom will a rose bush perish simply because it's planted in shade, but its blooms will be few and far between—if they are produced at all.

If your personal taste leans toward a formal look, Hybrid Teas will likely be your choice. Long, straight stems on upright plants give Hybrid Tea roses a formal appearance. They lend themselves well to planting along a fence line and also make good "background" plants. In a round or "island" garden, Hybrid Teas are very effective grouped in the center, with lower growing bushes around the perimeter. If you enjoy cut roses for the house or to give away, the stately beauty of Hybrid Teas is incomparable.

If there is any such thing as a grand order of roses, Grandifloras would probably come next in formality, both the blooms and the bushes. This classification is the result of crossing Hybrid Teas with Floribundas, creating cultivars that have distinct characteristics of both parents. These stately bushes may produce some long stems with one rose and other equally-long stems that sport two or more blooms. Like Hybrid Teas, Grandifloras are ideal for background plantings, along fences and as a center focal point for island gardens. It is not unusual for Grandifloras to reach six feet or more in height. 'Queen Elizabeth,' the first Grandiflora, is highly esteemed the world over.

Now we consider Floribundas, those short, dense bushes with masses of blooms that frequently produce sprays of up to nine blossoms. It seems safe to say that no other type of rose offers as much color as much of the time as Floribundas, and many that are classed as "ever-blooming" are truly that. Those considering using Floribundas in their landscape plan should know that not all Floribundas are "short and fat." 'Hannah Gordon,' 'Permanent Wave,' 'Lady of the Dawn,' 'Apricot Nectar' and 'Little Darling' are a few that aren't; they grow very tall and sprawling. Though they've earned their own special place in the garden, they should not be juxtaposed with low-growing Floribundas. Corners can be ideal for sprawling Floribundas, as can fencelines; they afford the bush something to lean on or be attached to. The growth habit of 'Little Darling' is more like a sprawling Climber or, in some instances, a pillar. Regardless, it is a purely delicious rose, with stems 18 to 20 inches long. A yellow blend, it's like a carved heap of peach ice cream, with a touch of strawberry. Its rich ivory-cream blends to golden yellow, splashed with rosy-pink. The stouter, more traditionally-formed Floribundas are ideal for borders along a walkway, a garden path, or around an island bed. They also make excellent potted plants for any location where there's ample sun.

Climbers, pillars, and Ramblers are ideal when used as background plantings. A chain-link fence can be turned into a thing of beauty with plantings of these roses, in a rainbow of colors or all one color. They bring great splashes of color to the garden throughout the seasons and they make ideal cut flowers, with stems that run the gamut in length from six inches to three feet. With regular pruning, Climbers and pillars can be kept to a reasonable height, so be sure to leave enough space for necessary pruning, as well as spraying and feeding.

The little princesses and princes of the rose world are, as their name implies, Miniatures. Their color range includes every primary color as well as every combination thereof. Miniatures are quite effective as border bushes, especially those not classed as the Mini-Miniatures, which are very small growers with equally small blooms. It is not unusual for some larger Miniatures to easily attain a height of two to three feet, more or less.

What color rose shall you choose? If complementary shades of color are important to you, consider bloom color when planning your landscape, combining pleasing, complementary colors.

THERESA ARTUSO on...
The Use of Roses in the Landscape

"There is no plant that offers so much flexibility or assumes so many different personalities as the rose. From a rambling climber on a garden trellis to a trained standard in a patio pot, the rose has many faces. Acclaimed for its varieties of fragrance, color and texture, there is an appropriate rose to be the carefully considered addition to any setting which offers minimum six hours sunlight daily.

"Everyone loves romance and there is nothing more romantic than the rose. Its floriferous beauty can prevent a design from looking too rough-hewn and allow keeping the plant palette simple. When cascading roses creep over a wall, the stone instantly seems ancient. Century-old heirloom roses can become the showpiece of a garden, offering a fresh take on tradition. People enjoy gardens that look as though they have been there forever.

"Paving and structures such as arbors, trellises, pergolas, terraces, benches and flights of steps organize a garden and create outdoor rooms. Roses can be used to accent these structures, drape an entry, flank a handsome gate and soften the edges of architectural outlines. When roses are selectively cut back from a trellis or arbor, the pleasing power of the structure comes to the foreground.

"One of the great legends of landscape design, Beatrix Farrand, refined the art of garden ornament and had strict rules to preserve the balance between architecture and greenery. She felt that no more than a third of the architectural surface should be covered with plant material. Delicate, routine pruning allows one to control the rose, if desired, to maintain this balance.

"Even its placement affords flexibility in the landscape. Softly spilling, cascading roses can be mixed with formal details. Often a sculpture or statue is the central, focal point of a manicured, circular rose garden. This round, continuous form reflects a Zen-like experience suggestive of the endless cycle of human existence.

"The selection of a particular variety of rose is often because of a personal connection, a past experience or, perhaps, even because of a description of it in a favorite poem. One's garden should be a reflection of one's passion and, often, if we are fortunate, memories and metaphor find expression in the landscape. In the words of the American writer, Gertrude Stein, 'A rose is a rose is a rose…' "

Although it's usually a mistake to buy a rose just for a pretty bloom, without seeing a flower it's impossible to fairly judge the color. For this reason, the best way to research rose cultivars is to visit gardens in your area to observe flower colors and habits of growth. When choosing from among unfamiliar roses, it's probably a mistake to take a garden center's word for color. Unless you are acquainted with a particular rose variety, don't buy it. Photographs on tags of roses are seldom realistic. Often, the tags are faded by weather, and even when new don't adequately convey the real color of the rose. If you must refer to photos, it's better to consult a reliable book on the subject.

Colonel Pease of Charlotte, North Carolina, dearly loved roses, so much so that at one time he called a nursery that specialized in them and ordered bushes to be planted in a garden at the front of his business. When asked "What variety?" He replied with a single word: yellow. His yellow rose garden flourished for years. He would not allow any other color to be planted. Years later, a friend at a local florist called him asking to "borrow" his sterling punch bowl. Being a generous gentleman, he lent the bowl as requested. The next day, on the occasion of his 100th birthday, the sterling silver bowl was returned—with one hundred yellow roses artistically arranged in it.

Another friend, who lived all his life in Charlotte and also loved roses, was speaking with me about various varieties, colors, et cetera. After a lot of discussion, he said, "Well, I know they're all beautiful and my wife loves all of them, but this garden is for me. I've been laying off to have a rose garden for years." He paused momentarily, then added, "You just pick out any and all the roses that you want to for my garden. But remember one thing: They all got to be red."

Fragrance is another consideration when trying to decide which roses to plant. After all, there's more than a rhyme to that old limerick, "The sweetest rose that grows is the rose that pleases the nose." Now, more than ever, there is such a wide group to choose from that no matter what color or classification you prefer, there's a sweet-smelling rose to delight the most particular grower. A fragrance is difficult to describe in words; no doubt, the most satisfactory way to select fragrant roses is to visit a garden center that specializes in roses, visit someone who grows them, or spend some time in a public garden, treating yourself to delicious scents there until you find the ones that please *your* nose.

Depending upon its location, whether or not a rose has thorns can be an advantage or a disadvantage. You may prefer that a bush growing near a path or gate be thornless, so that it won't scratch passersby or catch their clothing. On the other hand, a prickly rose hedge at the edge of your property might be just the thing to discourage trespassers. Nearly all roses have prickles, but some are thornier than others, and there are some thornless varieties, too.

Roses purchased from reputable dealers frequently have valuable information included on the identification tag regarding growth and habit. Also, detailed information covering all roses currently available in commerce is in the American Rose Society's *Handbook for Selecting Roses.* This booklet is crammed from cover to cover with all sorts of information about roses not found elsewhere in a single source. Probably the best first-hand information is yours, free for the asking, from American Rose Society (ARS) Consulting Rosarians and ARS Judges, who live and grow roses in every state in the Union. Names and addresses of Consulting Rosarians can be obtained from the American Rose Society.

In the quest for answers to which roses to choose, there are many factors to weigh. If after researching its characteristics, a rose loses its luster, you can always select another. There are thousands to choose from. Your search for the perfect bush may start with catalogs, then expand to include garden centers, discount stores, nurseries and backyard growers. As your needs and tastes change, so may your choice of roses, giving you opportunities to try new varieties.

Here by the pond the whisp'ring of wings...
Or is the morning beginning to sing?

OWN-ROOT ROSES

Primarily because of soil-borne nematodes, grafted roses are the norm in Florida. However, own-root roses do have advantages, and there are cultivars that can be grown here. The revered English gardener Gertrude Jekyll, author of the book *Roses for English Gardens,* profoundly believes that roses grow better and produce more prolifically on their own roots. The proprietors of Roses Unlimited of Laurens, South Carolina, a grower that produces only own-root bushes, shares this belief. Partner Pat Henry says, "There is no bud union to suffer winter kill, most varieties are long-lived, continually building strength because new basals develop directly from the root system, and no suckers are produced from a different root stock as with grafted roses." She adds, "The biggest advantage of grafted roses is that they give you a really big start in a hurry. Own-root roses start more slowly, catch up quickly and get better and better with time."

Ken Mayberger, a Southwest Florida hybridizer of heirloom roses, says emphatically that it is his experience that these roses grow better on their own roots than those that are grafted. Ken and his partner Penny Crawford should know. At their Naples nursery Roseglen Gardens, they have nearly 400 varieties which they have been growing for more than a dozen years. Laughing, Ken says, "I prune some of these with a chain saw!" Some that get the "chain saw treatment" include 'Louis Philippe,' developed in 1834 (AARS rating 8.6) and 'Mrs. B. R. Cant,' which made her debut in the world of roses just a century ago in 1901 (AARS rating 8.7). Roseglen Gardens also grows 'Fortuniana' rootstock roses and others, and they also specialize in daylily research and development.

Caring for own-root roses is the same as for grafted varieties. However, some cultivars are a little more susceptible to both diseases and insects, so in these cases a little more attention is required to identify and quickly treat problems.

The following article by Dr. Malcolm Manners, reprinted with permission from the November 1993 edition of *The Cherokee Rose* newsletter, is an excellent primer on own-root roses for Florida.

GRAFTED VS. OWN-ROOT ROSES
by Dr. Malcolm Manners

I've had several conversations with CFHRS [Central Florida Heritage Rose Society] members lately about the relative advantages and disadvantages of grafted and own-root roses. Much of what has appeared in print was written by authors in other climates and with different soil conditions than those of Central Florida. So I thought the subject might be worth an article.

First some concepts: The term "own-root" refers to roses that have been rooted from cuttings, divided, layered, tissue-cultured, or produced by some other method which caused a branch to produce roots of its own. In contrast, a grafted or budded plant is one in which a small piece of the desired flowering variety (the scion) was surgically attached to a root system from another rose (the rootstock, understock, or just "stock"). These two parts heal together to become a single plant. Budding is a type of grafting, and the terms are often used interchangeably. While methods of nursery production differ slightly, budded and grafted plants should behave identically in the garden, and any reference to "grafted" plants in this article is meant to include budded plants as well.

Own-root plants have some significant advantages over grafted plants. Own-root plants are usually cheaper, since they take less time to produce, as well as less skilled labor and often less total labor. Own-root plants also tend to live longer than grafted plants in a soil to which they are well adapted. Also, if an own-root plant freezes to the ground, it will usually sprout back out from below the soil surface. The sprouts are still the original variety, so you haven't lost the plant. So, in many areas of the country, you may find own-root bushes 50 or more years old, sometimes much more. However, if a grafted plant freezes to the graft union, the rootstock may sprout out but you will have lost the original grafted variety.

The biggest disadvantage of an own-root rose in Central Florida is that relatively few varieties are well adapted to our soil conditions. We have light, excessively well-drained, high-temperature soils, not at all ideal for most roses. While we can certainly improve the situation with the addition of generous amounts of organic matter, a problem we can't eliminate is nematodes—tiny worms in the soil. Most Florida soils are infested with many species of nematodes, some of which are entirely harmless, while others feed on plant roots. The most serious group on roses is the root knot nematodes (*Meloidogyne* spp.) If a rose is not resistant to these pests, it will not likely be successful on its own roots here. Roses are not either absolutely resistant or susceptible; rather there is wide variation from one rose cultivar to another in the level of resistance. Often, an own-root plant will grow rapidly and healthily here at first, then become less vigorous after a year or two, eventually becoming so unhealthy that it needs to be replaced. Others decline shortly after planting, while still others are highly resistant and may survive and thrive for many years.

The mere fact that a rose is grafted or budded does not insure that it is better adapted to a certain soil condition or more resistant to nematodes than an own-root rose would be. It is important to select a rootstock that is specifically adapted to your situation. It is by selecting a rootstock to match the local soil that one can obtain a plant that is superior to an own-root bush of the same variety. While many rootstocks have been tried, there are only five in common use in the United States.

'Multiflora' is a popular rootstock in Texas, Canada, and parts of the northeastern United States. It is not at all well adapted to Florida conditions, in that it apparently needs more winter chilling than we normally get and is highly susceptible to root knot nematodes. 'Multiflora'-rooted plants in Central Florida seldom thrive, even when first planted, and nearly always die by the third or fourth year. Florida growers would do well to avoid this stock. If you can't find a particular variety on any other root system, at least plan to transfer a scion to another stock as soon as possible from your 'Multiflora'-rooted plant.

'Manettii' is another stock sometimes encountered. Wayside Gardens sells plants on it; I'm not sure why. While not a terrible stock, it has little about it worth recommending for our climate or anyone else's. 'Manettii' is probably best used as an understock for greenhouse-grown roses.

By far the most commonly used stock in the United States, almost always produced in California, is 'Dr. Huey' (='Shafter'). A plant on 'Dr. Huey' roots tends to be a strong, healthy grower in Central Florida for the first five to six years. During this time, it grows and performs nearly as well as any other root system that we can use. However, after several years, the nematode population builds up to high enough levels that the plant can't replace roots as rapidly as they are being destroyed, and the plant declines. This process can be slowed down by using large quantities of organic matter in the planting hole and by keeping the bush deeply mulched, but ultimately, the plant will succumb to the nematode attack. It is rare to find a 'Dr. Huey'-rooted bush ten years old, or a really healthy one over five years old in Central Florida. So, Dr. Huey is an acceptable, even good, stock if you don't mind replacing your plants every few years. But if you want a long-lived plant, 'Dr. Huey' is not the best choice.

'Fun Jwan Lo,' a.k.a. 'Odorata' or 'Indica Major,' is a semi-tropical rootstock which is badly cold-damaged even here in Lakeland. In coastal South Florida, it has some strong proponents, since it seems to be rather forgiving of calcareous (high pH lime rock) soils, but I can't recommend it in areas that freeze. Also, in most areas of Florida, 'Fun Jwan Lo' tends to produce a less vigorous bush with fewer flowers than either 'Dr. Huey' or 'Fortuniana.' At least in our garden, it also produces far more suckers (sprouts from below the graft which have to be removed) than does any other stock we've tried. Its nematode tolerance appears to be similar to that of 'Dr. Huey.' 'Fun Jwan Lo' has the advantage of being unusually easy to root from cuttings, and to graft with a high degree of success.

'Fortuniana,' also sometimes known as 'Double Cherokee,' is currently the most popular rootstock in Florida. Note that it is not the same as the 'Cherokee Rose' (*R. laevigata*)… although the 'Cherokee Rose' is believed to have been one of the parents of 'Fortuniana.' 'Fortuniana' is semitropical and can be badly injured in a freeze, but it has been our experience that it is substantially more hardy than 'Fun Jwan Lo.' In the Christmas 1989 freeze, we lost nearly all our plants on 'Fun Jwan Lo,' but didn't lose any plants on 'Fortuniana' or 'Dr. Huey' roots. 'Fortuniana' is also the most nematode resistant of all our rootstocks, allowing it to grow vigorously for 30 or more years. No one knows exactly how long such bushes may thrive because grafted plants on 'Fortuniana' in the state are less than 40 years old, and some of them are still quite healthy. Plants on 'Fortuniana' are sometimes slower growing during the first few months after planting than plants on some other stocks, but once established, they quickly catch up with and surpass the growth of plants on any other root system. 'Fortuniana' makes a very far-reaching root system, extending out many feet from the bush. It is more drought-tolerant than any of our other common stocks, and it is able to extract fertilizer nutrients from a wide variety of soils. Plants on 'Fortuniana' ultimately grow to be unusually large. So, if you see an estimated height and/or width printed for a variety, you should assume that it will grow substantially bigger if grafted on 'Fortuniana' roots.

With any grafted plant, it is important to watch for suckers—stems growing out from the rootstock portion of the plant, below the graft. If allowed to grow, they will eventually crowd out the scion, and the graft will be lost. Many grafted plants are short-lived because no one bothers to de-sucker them. A convenient aspect of 'Fortuniana' is that its leaves are drastically different from those of most other roses, so suckers are easily recognized in the garden, even when quite small.

Considering all this, which type rose plant is best for a Central Florida garden? There are some roses which are excellent on their own roots. Some of the Chinas, for example, have been known to live 70 or more years here in Lakeland on their own roots. 'Old Blush,' 'Louis Philippe,' and 'Archduke Charles' are in this group of roses. Some Teas and Noisettes may also be grown for a number of years on their own roots, but I would caution you that in nearly ten years of searching, I have never found an own-root Noisette over five years old in the Lakeland area, nor have I found a Tea more than about that age, unless it was growing next to a concrete building or slab. On three occasions I've seen very old plants of 'Mrs. B. R. Cant' (a Tea) growing next to a building. We have a plant on campus that is at least 40 years old growing right next to a concrete sidewalk. Note that nematodes don't do well under heavy mulches, and in this case, concrete is a "heavy" mulch! We've never found any other own-root Tea in this area, regardless of its proximity to concrete. In addition to these roses ('Louis Philippe,' 'Archduke Charles,' 'Old Blush,' and 'Mrs. B. R. Cant'), here is a list of all the other roses I've ever found in Central Florida growing healthily on their own roots: 'Pink Pet' (supposedly a China; we may not have the real thing. Known as 'Caldwell Pink' in Texas), *R. laevigata* (the 'Cherokee Rose'); 'La Marne' (Polyantha); 'Spray Cécile Brünner' (Polyantha, also grown as 'Bloomfield Abundance'); and two plants of 'Tausendschön' (Hybrid Multiflora). Of course, big old plants of 'Fortuniana' are common, probably nearly always the remains of a formerly grafted plant. I wouldn't hesitate to recommend any of these roses on their own roots for this area of the State. But I would not recommend any other own-root roses for Central Florida, unless you know that the variety has been grown successfully for many years or unless you are willing to replace the plant fairly soon. If you want to gamble, other Chinas seem most likely to be successful, followed by some of the Teas. Somewhat north of here where the clay content of the soil is greater, the situation changes. Many roses do well there on their own roots. This is probably because root knot nematodes do not thrive on heavy, clay soils. But that is not the case on our sandy, non-clay-based soils.

I think it is a very important observation that you just don't see old own-root bushes of other varieties in this part of the State. There must be a reason for that, and I think it is that the plants have all died, due to their inability to adapt to our soil and pest conditions. Many people are planting Tea roses on their own roots in this area now. I wish them luck and success, but until those plants become several years old and are seen to be still thriving, I won't recommend own-root Teas for this area. I would always elect to put them on 'Fortuniana' roots, as I would all other roses not listed above.

One might ask if there are any disadvantages to a 'Fortuniana'-rooted bush in this area. I can think of only two: It maybe somewhat more cold-tender than an own-root plant, and it will require some sucker removal during the first few years. I don't consider either of these to be extreme disadvantages, and I think the advantages far outweigh them in most cases.

Note: If you are aware of an own-root rose in Central Florida not listed above, that you know to be more than 10 years old, please let me know about it. I'm interested in such roses.

'FORTUNIANA' ROOTSTOCK – ITS HISTORY AND VALUE

Upon the release of his book *Colorado*, James Michener was asked, "What exactly is your new book about?" Mr. Michener replied, "Well, in the first place, it's more about Colorado than you need know." Similarly, this chapter may be more than some rose growers need to know about 'Fortuniana' rootstock. All you really need to know is that the word "Fortuniana" on the next rose you purchase can make a big difference in the mature size of the bush and the flowers it produces in gardens where winters are mild. However, this chapter is for those who hunger for detailed information on a rootstock that continues to excel in producing bigger and better roses in temperate climates.

After more than a half-century of research and testing by University of Florida scientists, it is widely believed that *Rosa fortuniana* is the most successful rootstock for Florida. The horticulturists involved in its evaluation include the late Dr. Sam E. McFadden, horticulturist with the Agricultural Experiment Station, University of Florida in Gainesville, and individuals such as the late Mrs. Katy Lampkin of Bradenton, founder of the Bradenton Rose Society in 1956. 'Fortuniana' rootstock has also proven its hardiness by tolerating some cold weather, especially if it has had a chance to become acclimated. It is now being grown successfully in Georgia, South Carolina, North Carolina, Alabama, Louisiana, Mississippi, and Texas (with freeze protection). 'Fortuniana' rootstock roses are also being tried in gardens even farther west.

Aside from its value as a rootstock, 'Fortuniana' should not be overlooked for its own beauty. It throws out long, vigorous, graceful canes with relatively few prickles. Shiny, three-leaflet leaves are reminiscent of one of its alleged parents, the 'Cherokee Rose' (*R. laevigata*). Its white flowers are like those of its other alleged parent, the 'Lady Banks Rose' (*R. banksiae*), but are larger—about two inches across, and very double with a distinctive knot of petals in the center. Blooms have the fragrance of the 'Lady Banks Rose,' a delicate violet scent that carries well on the air. 'Fortuniana' blooms only in the spring, but it puts all its energy into a lavish and memorable display that can last for weeks. It exhibits a natural climbing growth but can also be pruned as a shrub, and is extremely disease resistant. As an own-root, landscape rose, 'Fortuniana' delighted and impressed its discoverer when he first encountered it over 150 years ago.

The story of 'Fortuniana' is a fascinating glimpse into the history of plant exploration and introduction. Its status today is due in no small measure to the horticultural knowledge and vision of many people who are also part of its story. We owe all of them a debt of gratitude for their persistence and dedicated love of roses.

Rosa fortuniana is thought to be a naturally-occurring hybrid of two species roses, *R. banksiae* and *R. laevigata*, both native to China. It is believed to have been discovered by a Scottish horticulturist named Robert Fortune (thus the name *Rosa fortuniana*) who found the double white rose growing in

Growing Roses with...
DIANE & JIM GILES

"Our rose nursery (Giles Nursery) is in Davenport, Florida, which is considered central Florida, more or less. We're located just off Interstate 4, west of Orlando.

"We grow our roses on 'Fortuniana' rootstock.

"Some of our most requested, best selling roses are 'Mr. Lincoln,' 'Double Delight,' 'Don Juan' and 'Belinda's Dream.' The reason these have continued consistently on our 'best-seller' list is that they grow and bloom so well year-in year-out.

"Over a period of years, we have found that most roses do not have a natural root system of their own that can absorb enough nutrients and water to produce enough food for the bush to produce big, beautiful blooms.

"The only way to get these big, beautiful roses everyone wants is to graft them onto a good sturdy root system which is 'Fortuniana.' 'Fortuniana' rootstock will grow roses faster, greatly increasing the size and quality of the flower not only in the South but also in mild regions that do not experience severe winter cold. Other good points about 'Fortuniana' are it's evergreen, and it's resistant to nematodes.

" 'Dr. Huey' has a short life-span in warm regions because it needs dormancy in the winter to rest.

"We've always grown Miniature roses, but now we're really excited about breeding our own. Minis, for the most part, are grown on their own rootstock, which is fine for Miniatures. However, there are some that we graft onto 'Fortuniana,' which produces superb bushes.

"And we're mighty happy to say that at the American Rose Society's National Rose Show in October 1998 in Charlotte, North Carolina, one of our own Miniatures, named 'Red Neck Girl,' was chosen to be placed on the Court of Honor. That was quite an honor for us! And we're also happy to say that yes, it is available now.

"So if growing roses is your love, we strongly advise that you start with 'Fortuniana' rootstock bushes. Keep them watered well, fertilize on a regular schedule and spray weekly.

"We live with the roses at our nursery and are open Tuesdays through Saturdays all year. Come to see us anytime… and always enjoy the roses!"

a Mandarin's garden in Ningpo, China, in 1848. In this same year, Fortune sent the rose back to England. Transporting delicate plants on long voyages by sea in those days was a special challenge, and Fortune was a pioneer in using the "Wardian Case" for this purpose. This airtight glass case, invented by N. B. Ward, kept plants in a sealed, moist atmosphere much like a modern terrarium. In a letter at that time Fortune describes his find: "The white climbing rose referred to is cultivated in gardens about Ningpo and Shanghai, and it is held in high esteem by the Chinese; indeed it is one of the best white kinds which I have ever met with in China. It is a luxuriant grower, blooms profusely and is no doubt well worth cultivation in English gardens."

In 1850, two years after its discovery in China, the English botanist John Lindley introduced *Rosa fortuniana*, which he had named in Robert Fortune's honor, to the Royal Horticultural Society. One year later, 'Fortuniana' is first described in *Paxton's Flower Garden*, by Sir Joseph Paxton with the same John Lindley, published in London. In 1852, a major horticultural reference work was published in France, *Le Jardin Fleurites*, by C. H. LeMaire. LeMaire's description of *Rosa fortuniana* is an exact translation from the Paxton-Lindley book from English to French, except that LeMaire uses an incorrect formation into Latin of the name Fortune, introducing the epithet "Fortuneana." So, from the beginning, depending on which work was referenced, there came into use two spellings for the same rose. Unfortunately, the incorrect spelling became the more commonly used one. To us today, this might seem like a simple and insignificant mistake, but in fact it began the dilemma of this rose being identified by many different names, none of them the correct one.

When Robert Fortune sent *Rosa fortuniana* back to England, he thought it would thrive in every English garden. He had an unbounded enthusiasm for every plant he discovered, especially "his" rose, but after languishing for many years, trying to become established in English outdoor gardens, 'Fortuniana' was deemed too tender to survive English winters. It was, however, kept in quantity in the great palm house and in the temperate house at Kew Gardens. At the time, both of these houses were unsurpassed as centers of scientific study and research for botanists and scholars from around the world.

Around 1900, England began sending 'Fortuniana' out to other countries in response to requests for a rootstock that might perform well in temperate climates. There is an early mention (1903) of 'Fortuniana' being sent to the Perth area of Western Australia. Although grafted roses were not nearly as common then as they are today, 'Fortuniana' had already been introduced into the southeastern United States. 'Fortuniana' is believed to have first gone to the Fruitland Nursery at Augusta, Georgia, and from there to the Glen St. Mary Nursery in Florida. The Glen St. Mary Nursery was founded by George L. Taber and his family in 1882, and produced a complete horticultural plant catalog from 1888 until 1950. In the 1894 catalog they began offering grafted roses. 'Cécile Brünner' was among the first offered. In 1906, Dr. Harold Hume joined Glen St. Mary Nursery. He was a professor at the University of Florida, Gainesville, and an early advocate of grafted roses over own-root roses.

By the time Robert Fortune discovered *R. fortuniana* in China, one of its two alleged parents had already made its way to the southeastern United States, having been brought there by early settlers. They called *Rosa laevigata,* a single white rose with five petals growing untended in the wild, the 'Cherokee Rose.' *Rosa fortuniana*, offspring of the 'Cherokee Rose' but with a many-petalled bloom, was called 'Double Cherokee' by some and 'Evergreen Cherokee' by others. *Rosa banksiae,* 'Fortuniana's other parent, has its own history and is established as the 'Lady Banks Rose,' a variety of which is also known as the 'Yellow Rose of Texas.'

As we can begin to understand, the proper name and accurate identification of *R. fortuniana* became a muddle. The picture that emerges from its beginnings in this country is of a rose known by several different names or by its proper name—misspelled. Add to this a lessening of interest in the variety, because it was expensive and difficult to propagate, and at that time growing roses on their own roots was more accepted. The lack of concern for anyone to set the facts straight also becomes understandable. Interest faded and 'Fortuniana' became a forgotten rose.

In 1963, the founder and editor of the Bradenton Rose Society, Mrs. Katy Lampkin, wrote about the "amazing comeback of a star, *Rosa fortuniana,* and its use as a rootstock for Florida roses." In her article, Katy refers to the 1921 *American Rose Annual,* in which Dr. H. H. Hume (associated with Glen St. Mary Nurseries) praises the qualities of 'Fortuniana' as a rootstock, but also explains the difficulties he encountered in propagating it during fifteen years of testing, problems that limited its commercial availability. Katy also states that she was introduced to 'Fortuniana' when she purchased her first roses from Glen St. Mary Nursery some 30 years before, in the early 1930s.

A year earlier, in 1962, Katy Lampkin had written, in collaboration with her friend and colleague Dr. Sam E. McFadden, describing a new method of grafting roses "by which the union between scion (desired hybrid variety) and the rootstock takes place during the time the cutting is rooting under a fine mist of water." This had not been done before. Katy's writing continues: "Since *Rosa fortuniana* has proven so adaptable to Florida's climate and sandy soils, and shows resistance to crown gall and certain nematodes, by all means obtain some cuttings of this rootstock. It's also known as 'Double Cherokee' or just 'Fortuniana.' If it is not available in your area, then *Rosa odorata,* 'Dr. Huey' or *Rosa multiflora* could be substituted. Dr. Sam suggests that a beginner might be more elated with the faster rooting results of any of these three but agrees that the 'Fortuniana' root is well worth waiting for. It will usually take from four to five weeks for the 'Fortuniana' to root, while the others will root in three."

Thus the tide had turned for *Rosa fortuniana!*

Not long afterwards, Katy Lampkin wrote that Dr. Sam deserved all the medals for the comeback of 'Fortuniana' and attributed the greatest boost to

A field of Rosa fortuniana *blooming at Nelsons' Florida Roses.*

his development of rooting rootstock cuttings under mist. Katy said, "Certainly knowing this rootstock had been used commercially years ago helped." This fact, remembered by very few, stayed with Katy because she still had roses growing in her Bradenton garden on the 'Fortuniana' stock obtained from Glen St. Mary Nurseries 30 years earlier. Some of those had almost attained the size of a small cottage!

From long experience, Katy could state, "So far, I know of no variety which has not been just as good on *R. fortuniana* as on any other, and most varieties are better on it." Also of value, she adds, "While growth and productivity from *R. fortuniana* are good from the start, it really is from the second year on that it shows its true worth."

The second important part of the 'Fortuniana' comeback story involves a letter from Mr. J. R. Sealy, Director of the Royal Botanical Garden in England, to Dr. McFadden at the University of Florida, stating that the proper spelling of Robert Fortune's rose was *"fortuniana,"* and that LeMaire's deliberate change to *"fortuneana"* in his translation over a hundred years before revealed his lack of scholarship and knowledge of Latin. Unfortunately, the LeMaire spelling had come into common usage in this country, used by the American Rose Society in all editions of *Modern Roses* that listed 'Fortuniana' up to that time. It is probably no surprise that Katy

Lampkin is credited with leading the initiative that brought about the proper correction.

Roses grafted onto 'Fortuniana' rootstock are now widely available all over the state. And now, unlike a few years ago, there are hundreds of varieties, including Tea Roses, Floribundas, Grandifloras, Climbers and numbers of Old Garden and English cultivars and even some Miniatures.

Now that 'Fortuniana' is being successfully grown in "cold" climate gardens, its importance is even more significant. As with any grafted/budded rose ('Dr. Huey' or others) grown in cold climates, the bud union/graft must be provided with winter protection.

It is widely, and inaccurately, believed that 'Fortuniana' is native to Florida. It's not difficult to understand why, for as one botanist observed, just one misinterpretation can throw off years of research and scientific findings. Regardless of 'Fortuniana' not being a native, it is well adapted to Florida soils and climates. Perhaps taking poetic license, it can be said that 'Fortuniana' is "nearly native" by virtue of its adoption so many years ago.

Little could Robert Fortune have imagined how valuable his finding of *Rosa fortuniana* was destined to be. Its future as an understock certainly could not have been on his mind when he first discovered it, but rose growers in Florida and other temperate regions can be glad he did. It has changed and continues to change rose growing culture in the South and elsewhere as more rosarians learn about its advantages and virtues.

The rose said: "Come to the garden and see...
There's something sweet 'tween thee and me."

Growing Roses with... MARK NELSON

"Following in the footsteps of my father, I have been in this rose-growing business for a good bit of my lifetime—long enough to know that roses can require a bit more care, in some instances, than other landscape plants; however, the rewards make any extra work well worth the effort.

"There are so many different roses and each one that comes along seems to be more beautiful than preceding ones, which all goes to make selecting just a few quite difficult. We have found that it is very helpful to visit public gardens, as well as private ones of people who have grown them successfully. And when I say 'visit private ones' I certainly am thinking of that vast number of rose fans who grow a dozen varieties, more or less, and who wish and work for more!

"One of the better public rose gardens in Florida is Orlando's Leu Gardens, which includes vast numbers of varieties and species that will show shapes, colors, sizes and forms that no photographs can show. And then, there's the fragrance, which is piquing the interest of more and more people.

"As you begin or continue to grow roses, no doubt questions will arise about their care… what to do or not to do. Members of the Central Florida Rose Society are always happy to talk about roses and to help others succeed in growing them. These members meet at the Garden House at Leu Botanical Gardens on the first Wednesday of the month. The Orlando Area Historical Rose Society meets the first Sunday of each month at 3:00 PM at the gardens. I can assure you, these rose lovers are always happy to help others who want to share their enthusiasm for the world's most popular flower.

"Rose help is also available at the Orange County Extension Service, as well as at other County Extension Offices. Also, telephone questions are welcomed and answered. Free Extension bulletins on home rose culture are available.

"In the interest of furthering the growing and enjoyment of roses, we at Nelsons' Florida Roses are always happy to help with information and advice about the world's most honored flower.

"The joy and rapture of roses. No other flower in the world inspires as does the rose, the oldest flower known to mankind."

After the deep of night
The first streaks of light…
Shhh… a rose is being born.

'FORTUNIANA' FIRST, 'DR. HUEY' SECOND

If we name 'Fortuniana' as our number one choice, 'Dr. Huey' would have to be our next-favorite rootstock. Roses grafted onto 'Dr. Huey' grow well in Florida and produce fine blooms, even though the bushes do not attain the size of those grafted onto 'Fortuniana.' Usually they have a much shorter lifespan, and often demonstrate a dislike for year-round performance, since 'Dr. Huey' by its nature takes kindly to winter dormancy. If grown as an own-root rose, 'Dr. Huey' produces clusters of showy, crimson, semi-double blooms.

Although we rate 'Dr. Huey' second-best, if we cannot find a variety we particularly want on 'Fortuniana' rootstock, we do not hesitate to buy a 'Dr. Huey' bush. A case in point: Our neighbor Lynn Woods called one day, saying, "The rose 'Secret' you cannot live without"—and thus the search began. It did not take many phone calls to learn that 'Secret,' an extraordinary, pink-shaded Hybrid Tea, was unavailable on 'Fortuniana' rootstock at that time. Our calls did, however, turn up four bushes on 'Dr. Huey,' so we bought them—sight unseen! When we made the trek to Treasure Island Garden Center in Okeechobee to pick them up, we were astounded at the size of the plants, foliage quality, and general first class condition, each bush having dozens of both buds and blooms. These were container-grown bushes, as almost all Florida roses are at point of purchase. They were in five- and seven-gallon containers, which undoubtedly contributed to their size and quality, as did the growing expertise of Young Rucks, owner of Treasure Island Garden Center.

These 'Secret'/'Dr. Huey' roses have now been in our garden for nearly three years. In the meantime, we did find a small 'Fortuniana' bush, so now we have this stunning cultivar on two rootstocks. The 'Fortuniana' bush, though at least two years younger than the 'Dr. Huey' plants, has very nearly caught up with them.

The following, from *The Rose: An Encyclopedia of North American Roses, Rosarians, and Rose Lore* by Sean McCann, is used with the kind permission of Stackpole Books, 5067 Ritter Road, Mechanicsburg, PA 17055.

'Dr. Huey'

This dark red rose won lasting fame as a stock for propagation.

The name of leading Philadelphia amateur rosarian in the 1920s, dentist Robert Huey, remains very much alive today because of this rose. It was bred in 1914 by Captain George C. Thomas and named in honor of the man who started him in roses. At the time of its national introduction in 1919, it was regarded as the darkest red of all climbing roses. J. Horace McFarland wrote that it was a "unique variety which carries its abundant June flowers without any fading into bluish shades." And although 'Dr. Huey' was widely accepted for itself, it became famous in a very different way.

A search was on for suitable understock in a budding trial in California, and 'Dr. Huey' was included in the trial by mistake. But it was the easy overall winner and has since been used to propagate millions of roses. Ironically—as Trenholm N. Meyer pointed out in the American Rose Society annual of 1991—just before this special use of 'Dr. Huey' was discovered, Captain Thomas had written an article for the American Rose Society (1922) in which he entered the debate on the best way to propagate roses, by budding or from cuttings. Thomas believed that while a great many roses could be successfully propagated on their own roots, all roses could be successfully budded. But he pointed out that "the best stock for every variety has not yet been listed." Little did he know that his own dark red rose would solve the problem for the majority of American rose growers.

I heard the rose say, "It's a bluebird day,"
Then I knew Spring was on the way...

CLASSIFICATIONS & VARIETIES OF ROSES

Over time, roses from different classes have been crossed and recrossed to the point that countless "modern" roses are not of pure strain. Their mixed parentage gives them traits from a number of different groups, complicating the classification of roses so that divisions are cloudy and the task is all but impossible.

One notable example is 'Apricot Nectar.' At the time it was developed, this highly fragrant, apricot cultivar was classified as a Floribunda. Some years later, that classification was officially changed to Hybrid Tea and even later it was designated as a Climber. The truth is that it has strong characteristics of all three classes! Some time ago, it was returned to its original designation of Floribunda. Apparently its breeder, the renowned German Mr. Gene Boerner, was right 35 years ago when he introduced this extraordinary apricot blend into the world of roses as a Floribunda.

Worldwide rose authority Sean McCann writes, "regarding the classification of roses… it is a subject for a lifetime's discussion and one that starts many an argument. Perhaps the words of J. Horace McFarland should be heeded, who said many years ago that 'general agreement upon classifications in this much-mixed genus is apparently an impossible dream.' Different countries go different ways and even within countries there are variations. The ARS declares there are 56 variations, the British Association of Rose Breeders reduced this number to 30, the World Federation of Rose Societies argues every three years about its suggested 37 classifications."

Following are some of the major classifications of roses recognized by the American Rose Society. For simplicity, the more obscure classes have been omitted.

OLD GARDEN ROSES (OGR): These roses have been "resurrected and rescued" from the gardens of yesterday, some dating as far back as the early 1700s. These include 'Abricote,' 'Alexandra,' 'Duke of York,' 'Little Gem,' 'Old Blush,' 'Green Rose,' et cetera. It's been said that Old Garden Roses have no form. However form, like beauty, may be in the eye of the beholder. Many are full and somewhat

'Green Rose' is an interesting, unusual example of an Old Garden Rose.

frilly, fluffy and sometimes floppy, with big heavy heads. They grow free-form, in all directions, not unlike many Polyanthas (see below). Into this group also fall sub-classifications such as the Bourbons, Centifolias, Chinas, Moss Roses, Noisettes, Gallicas, Damasks, and others.

SHRUB ROSES (S): In this group are the Classic Shrubs and the Modern Shrubs. The Classic Shrubs bear family names. Back in the 1700s many European rulers, including English, French and Spanish royalty, sent their people out over the world looking for roses. Those that were brought back to the respective countries were propagated and given family names that have survived down through the years. One of the most celebrated families in "rose circles" was that of Napoleon and his wife Josephine. 'Hybrid Rugosa' is a Shrub Rose, as are 'Belinda's Dream,' 'Bonica,' and 'Carefree Beauty.' Modern Shrubs, such as the David Austin roses, have been developed more recently from the Classics and for simplicity are known as Modern Shrubs.

POLYANTHAS (POL): These roses exhibit a many-stemmed growth pattern with clusters of blooms, and are both old and new. Although there are small Polyanthas, most grow tall and wide, branching prolifically.

HYBRID TEA (HT): Hybrid Teas have a classic, formal, shapely bloom and were first developed from the crossings of rose species discovered in China and elsewhere. Typically, Hybrid Teas are borne on long stems, often with several side buds, each flower having 30 to 50 petals. The modern era of the elegantly-formed Hybrid Tea was born in 1945 with

*'Sun Flare' Floribunda (left) and
'Olympiad' Hybrid Tea (right)*

the introduction of 'Peace,' whose public appearance and praise was so dramatically overwhelming that its place in rose history was instantaneous.

FLORIBUNDA (F): This classification includes many-flowering varieties with clusters of buds and blooms on each stem. Floribundas are used widely in landscaping and for great splashes of color in the garden.

GRANDIFLORA (GR): This classification emerged as a result of a highly successful mating of 'Floradora' (F) and 'Charlotte Armstrong' (HT). The resulting rose not only exhibited the characteristics of a Hybrid Tea, but also the ability to bear clusters—or "trusses"—of blooms, and to grow six feet (or more) in height. Thus, in 1954 the class of Grandiflora was born, with 'Queen Elizabeth' having the distinction of being the first member of the class. Its medium-pink buds are pointed, high-centered to cupped, borne singly and in clusters. The latter characteristic has proven to be a dependable trait of Grandifloras that grow straight and upright.

RAMBLERS (R), CLIMBERS (C) AND LARGE FLOWERED CLIMBERS (LCL): These groups of roses are defined by their growth habits rather than by their parentage. They include climbing Bourbon, China, Floribunda, Grandiflora, Hybrid Tea and other roses. "Pillar roses" are also included and are considered Large Flowered Climbers. They have canes that are sturdier and more self-supporting than Climbers or Ramblers, but are otherwise similar. 'Don Juan,' the most widely-grown rose in Florida, is officially classified as a Large Flowered Climber and may also be referred to as a pillar rose. Many times 'Don Juan' does, in fact, exhibit strong characteristics of pillar roses, but it is not unusual for two bushes planted side-by-side to grow with distinctly different habits. One may have all the characteristics of a pillar, while the other grows as a very tall, traditional Climber.

MINIATURE AND MINIATURE-FLORA (MIN. AND MINI-FLORA): Due to their novelty, versatility and very modest space requirements, these small roses have increased dramatically in popularity. Not only are they used for edgings, planted extensively in rock gardens, and grown in containers, they are widely used for temporary decoration indoors. Mini-Flora roses are a new classification adopted by the American Rose Society in 1999, and are larger than traditional miniatures. Their designation marks another step in the evolution of the rose, with their intermediate size falling between that of Miniatures and Floribundas.

The group of roses dubbed "patio roses," which most of the world does not accept as a classification, is the result of crossing Miniatures with Floribundas. In some cases, patio roses are produced by laboriously crossing the largest Miniatures with other large Miniatures, then crossing and re-crossing the largest of the resulting roses again and again. The result, as you would suspect, are roses that appear to be neither Miniature nor the size of most Floribundas.

WHICH ARE THE MOST PROLIFIC PERFORMERS?

Although we live some 15 miles from Ace Garden Center in LaBelle, and over 40 from Scrivner's Nursery & Garden Center, an independent, full-time, full-line plant operation which has been serving garden enthusiasts for over 20 years in Fort Myers, I spend as much time as possible in both. After all, they share our passion for roses and understand the necessity for feeding the habit. Sadly enough, such operations—those with knowledgeable personnel who care about their plants and the people they serve—have become endangered and are all but extinct. This is not a vendetta against plant departments of discount chains and supermarkets, but a declaration of support for independent garden centers and nurseries that are fast fading from the American scene. If discount plant

'Brigadoon' Hybrid Tea

dealers had reasonable knowledge and information about their nursery stock, and if they gave reasonable care to their plants—even things as elementary as keeping them watered—it would be a different matter. Even so, I admit to occasionally visiting such places; it is my nature to stop and admire any beautiful plant noticed in passing. If there's a purely outstanding bloom, even one not identified, I don't hesitate to buy it—at a cut-rate price, of course.

One such rose was so extraordinary that we took it home and added it to our garden even though the plant was in poor condition. The soil in the pot was dry as cotton and the leaves were dehydrated, but the lovely bloom caught my eye and heart. It was just perfect—creamy white, with deep pink edging. In pencil, the bush was labeled 'Polk's Delight,' with no other information. This name was not included in the *Handbook for Selecting*

'Secret' Hybrid Tea

Roses, nor could any ARS judge who saw the rose identify it. We knew from looking at the grafted joint that it was not on 'Fortuniana' rootstock but we could not determine whether it was 'Dr. Huey' or 'Multiflora.' Judging from the bush's lack of stamina and the way it was grafted, we suspect it was 'Multiflora.' In a few months it went into a steady state of decline and in spite of all our ministrations, it died.

Fortunately, we had taken cuttings and asked Mel Bough to graft them onto 'Fortuniana' rootstock, a task he does superbly. Mel's grafted bushes proved that the rose itself was superb. It turned out to be a Climber, with cycles of blooms akin to those of 'Don Juan.' Unfortunately, we lost our bush along with sixty-some others when downy mildew struck several years ago, but we gave Lynn Woods one of Mel's grafted plants and it is still thriving in her garden.

We never learned this rose's rightful name and have often wondered if it could have been a seedling or even a sport. For our private identification, we named it 'Captain's Delight.' It was reminiscent of an old, old cultivar called 'Kordes Perfecta.' However, 'Kordes Perfecta' has more petals and its picot edging is not so pronounced, nor is the coloring of the edging as intense a pink. The form of 'Captain's Delight' was exquisitely perfect. From new bud to completely open rose, every creamy-white, pointed petal was unexcelled.

'First Prize' Hybrid Tea

'Captain's Delight'

When we visit with the folks at either of the two garden centers that are our usual haunts, we invariably swap opinions on the roses that are the "biggest and best and that perform the most" in this region. They and we totally agree that a rose that performs wonderfully for us may not do the same in a garden a block or a mile away. Many factors are involved. For instance, two bushes of the same variety, purchased at the same time and at the same place, may be vastly different. Even though one may be a strong vigorous bush and the other may be weak, it's entirely possible for them to superficially look the same. Also, soil conditions from one garden to another vary widely, as does exposure. So for bushes to be compared accurately, they must be reasonably the same, but they also must be grown under the same conditions and given the same care and treatment. Even so, seldom do we talk with others who already grow roses (or who are about to start) that the question does not arise, "But which varieties bloom the most?"

Our answer always includes 'Don Juan,' 'Secret,' 'Cécile Brünner,' 'Lady of the Dawn,' 'Brigadoon,' 'Belinda's Dream' and 'St. Patrick.' There are others that perform magnificently at special times of the year. 'Ballerina' is glorious in February but rarely does anything to speak of the rest of the year! 'Elegant Beauty' follows a pattern that you could set your watch by; every three to four weeks, almost the entire bush bursts into extraordinary, long-stemmed, long-budded blooms unlike any other in the garden. Down the road a short distance, Diana Richards declares that no other rose she has ever grown has ever bloomed as much or as often as 'Carefree Beauty.'

Five Floribundas that outproduce any we've ever grown are 'Sun Flare,' 'Angel Face,' 'Diadem,' 'Hannah Gordon' and 'Permanent Wave.' Their recycling is remarkably fast and dependable. All five are fine for cutting when picked as true buds, as opposed to half buds. 'Sun Flare' is not as long-lasting as 'Angel Face,' either as a cut rose or on the bush, and its buttercup-yellow faces tend to droop a little by the second or third day. However, its petals stay intact and present a pretty contrast in color and form in bouquets.

Almost everyone who grows them agrees that there are some roses that are just plain stingy bloomers, but among these misers are some of the most striking varieties—roses like 'Dolly Parton,' 'Tansinnroh/Joyfulness,' 'Cary Grant,' and 'White Masterpiece.' And who is not thrilled at the sight of 'Pristine' or 'First Prize'? We have seen much better performances of these two in some other gardens, but alas, they are not among our best bloomers. Even so, we would not willingly be without either of them and therefore, we wait—though not patiently—for their magnificent blooms.

In an ofttimes harsh and harrowing world,
Shadows fall gently on the rose.

CHANGING WITH THE SPANNING OF SEASONS

When the calendar rolls around to October, those of us who grow roses wonder why we don't have twice as many. Somehow, beginning in mid-autumn, Mother Nature seems to make all things work together for good in the Florida rose garden. Bushes take on renewed vigor and stamina, growing taller and wider. Longer nights cause buds to develop more slowly, thus they attain a much larger size before opening; the blooms unfurl at a more leisurely pace, with finer form and more intense colors.

There may be no more dramatic example of this than the world's most honored rose, 'Peace.' In a Florida spring, 'Peace' is soft yellow, blushed with pink on the edges of its outer petals. In the heat of midsummer, the blooms are much smaller, the yellow becoming paler with only the slightest trace of pink. But come the longer nights and cooler temperatures of autumn, 'Peace' takes on breathtaking shadings: rich gold and intense pink. Even though

'Peace' is a very full-petalled rose, through the gentle fall and winter seasons of Florida her petals hold themselves exquisitely upright, and there are too many of them to count.

Another rose that differs significantly in autumn is 'Cécile Brünner.' Although not officially classed as an antique rose, 'Cécile Brünner' was developed over a hundred years ago and remains a favorite among many growers, including us. Its naturally petite size only adds to its charm. Pure, light-pink blooms are borne on long, graceful stems that may be 12 to 18 inches in length. Even with regular cutting, our 'Cécile' boasts heavy foliage year-round, growing six feet tall and just as wide. Its form is remarkably similar to that of large Hybrid Teas, and its petals are held upright for several days. When fully open, 'Cécile Brünner' is a perfectly-formed pompon powder puff. During high spring and summer, she is a pale, delicate, pearl pink—but in autumn her dress is anything but pale. As the

Friend and neighbor Joe Flint dearly loves all of nature's creatures here in the backwoods of Glades County. When he first saw this photograph, he held it at arm's length and with a serenely hushed expression said, "Peace, Oh Perfect Peace"—so that became its title! Little frog (Hyla squirella) *wins friends every day in the rosary, feeding on tiny insects but leaving nary a blemish on even the most delicate petals. 'Peace' Hybrid Tea is one of the best-known and most celebrated roses of all time.*

27

year wanes, her outer petals become a deep, rich pink, slightly veined, and the bloom is about one-third larger than in spring and summer.

The relatively new, totally spectacular 'St. Patrick' Hybrid Tea, an All-America Rose Selections (AARS) winner, is commonly spoken of as a "green rose." Well, in my "coloring book," 'St. Patrick' cannot be called green, as such. Yet, in fall and winter, and even in early spring, the undersides of its outer petals are very definitely brushed with green and somewhat veined, while the rest of its petals are rich, lemon yellow. In the 1998 *Handbook for Selecting Roses,* 'St. Patrick' is classed as a yellow blend, and although the blend color is not specified, one can assume that the reference is to green. The brush of green is not dominant on the outer petals of 'St. Patrick,' yet it is totally striking, as is the outstanding form of the rose, and of the bush as well.

There's something else unusual about 'St. Patrick' in our garden. Our two bushes, from different growers, are located in the same general area of the garden, about ten feet apart. Since the first bloom appeared on each bush, their colors have been noticeably different, even though we see no difference in bud, or flower form, or size. One is soft lemon yellow, while the other is a rich golden yellow, and it is the lemon-yellow rose that exhibits the most green on the outer petals.

'China Green' *(R. chinensis viridiflora),* an Old Garden Rose is known by various names and is truly pure green. "Old" it really is, according to *Modern Roses 9* published by the American Rose Society which notes that 'China Green' was cultivated prior to 1845. Of all the bushes in our garden, this one demands the least pruning attention. Its blooms are usually 1^1/$_2$ to 2 inches wide. Both single and candelabras are borne on a bush that grows dense and low, about 2^1/$_2$ feet tall. The totally scentless blooms are full, each petal is held high, and the blossoms somewhat resemble small

'St. Patrick'
Hybrid Tea

chrysanthemums. There are many who say 'China Green' doesn't even look like a rose—nevertheless, a rose it is, with typical, traditional rose foliage. Its rating is 7.3, and it is eligible for Dowager Queen.

We have only one 'China Green' bush, a gift from Mel and Rita Bough. Mel rooted it, an art in which he excels. The freeze did not faze it—not buds, blooms nor foliage—and now it has a full dress of new growth and too many ready-to-bloom buds to count.

There seems to be no middle ground for liking or disliking 'China Green.' It's either loved or hated. We are in the "love" group for many reasons, not the least of which is its unfading emerald green color. As a cut rose, it's incomparable, and it has the shortest recycling period of any rose in the garden. I've always been partial to using it as a filler rose, combining it with 'Sun Flare,' 'Cécile Brünner,' 'Little Darling' and many others. These small roses come close to arranging themselves.

Frail pink petals lay in my palm like a prayer…
Smiling at their fragrance
Old worries wafted away.

'Paradise' Hybrid Tea (left) and 'Angel Face' Floribunda (right).

BLACK 'N' BLUE — AN INCOMPLETE PALETTE

Five of the basic colors of the rainbow—violet, green, yellow, orange, and red—are well represented in the rose garden. The palette of roses includes those that shade from white to red as they open, those that open as one color, then pale to near-white, and others that are distinctly striped or splotched with two or more colors. Of the seven rainbow colors, those that are missing in roses are indigo and blue. Also missing is black, not really a color at all, but an absence of it.

Various catalogs, newsletters, and "on the road" rose salesmen praise their roses in general and these out-of-the-ordinary colors in particular. Much has been written, shown and said about roses in hues that do not exist in reality. Some catalogs show photographs that obviously have been colored or manipulated by artificial means. But there are no black roses, nor blue ones. This is not a matter of opinion. In the rose world, a great deal of research in breeding continues to take place, but so far there's no cultivar that's true black, nor is there one that's true blue.

The cultivar that's nearest to black is an old, large-flowered Hybrid Tea named 'Zulu Queen.' It has a superb, high bud center and is a very deep, dark shade of red with strong fragrance. However, the tips of the petals quickly discolor to a grayish-black color that's very unattractive, and the bush is a stingy bloomer. At one time, 'Zulu Queen' was advertised as "the black rose," but at this writing we've not been able to find anyone growing it, and it's not listed in any of the last 20 years' issues of the *Handbook for Selecting Roses*. Thus, it is probably safe to assume that 'Zulu Queen' is no longer considered in commerce, although there are a few commercial rose growers that specialize in obscure, hard-to-find cultivars. Another variety that's frequently been called "black" is 'Oklahoma,' but its large flowers are actually a very dark red.

As for roses called "blue," these range in color from lilac to lavender and other purplish hues. There are a number of them, the most touted probably being 'Blue Girl'/'Kolner Karneval.' In all honesty, it would take more imagination than I have to call this rose blue. The ones we've seen are an unlovely shade of lavender. Some of the other "blue" cultivars are exceptional, however, three of them being 'Angel Face' (F), rated by AARS at 7.8, 'Paradise' (HT), with an AARS rating of 7.1, and the old Hybrid Tea cultivar 'Sterling Silver.' The latter, although very pale, was one of the very first in this color range and as a result caused quite a stir in the first few years of its existence. 'Sterling Silver' is listed as a mauve rose. It's a stingy performer, which contributes to its low AARS rating of 4.1. Considering this and other factors, it doesn't claim

'Pristine' Hybrid Tea

Mist' (Min), 'Blue Moon' (HT), 'Blue Nile' (HT), 'Blue Peter' (Min), 'Blue Ribbon' (HT), 'Blue River' (HT), 'Blue Skies' (HT), 'Blue Violet' (HT), 'Blueberry Hill' (F), 'Blueblood' (Min). Of course, there are others and more are being introduced.

This discussion brings to mind a florist that without fail advertised the availability of both black and blue roses. One fine day my curiosity got the better of me and I went in to look around. Sure enough, there were both black roses and blue ones in the cooler.

Of course, they had been sprayed with florist's spray paint, and the slashed-mashed stems had been placed in black-dyed water or blue-dyed water for a day or so. The florist explained that turning white roses into blue ones is easier than turning white to black, but she said "You just never know what a customer will ask for so we do whatever we can to satisfy each and ever' one that walks in our door!" She went on to say that when black roses are requested, most of the time the darkest red ones are sprayed black, adding "We don't have too many who come in and ask for black or blue roses, but those that do seem to be satisfied—so far."

a spot in our garden, but will always claim a spot in our hearts since it was Mama's favorite rose until 'Pristine' made its way into the world of roses.

Here are some other cultivars that make their claim as blue roses in name, if not in color: 'Blue Bajou' (F), 'Blue Bell' (HT), 'Blue Boy' (S), 'Blue Chip' (F), 'Blue Crystal' (Min), 'Blue Heaven' (HT), 'Blue Ice' (Min), 'Blue Magic' (Min), 'Blue

He knows the sweetest rose...
Hummingbird... he's kissed them all.

SPORTS: GRAND SURPRISES IN THE GARDEN

What exactly is a sport? According to Webster's International Unabridged Dictionary (1937), a sport is:

"a sudden spontaneous deviation or variation from type; a mutation (1); an individual organism which differs from its parents beyond the usual limits of individual variation. Specifically, in botany, a bud variation.

"(1) A sudden variation, the offspring differing from its parents in some well-marked character or characters as distinguished from a gradual variation in which the new characters become highly developed only in the course of many generations."

In the world of roses, there are many extraordinary sports, both celebrated and unknown. A few that are particularly exceptional include 'Chicago Peace' (sport of 'Peace'), 'Fountain Square' (sport of 'Pristine'), and 'Magic Lantern' (sport of 'Gold Medal').

A relatively unknown, but beautiful sport was "born" in the garden of Lynn and Rusty Woods. This one occurred on 'Bon-Bon,' a bush that we had given the Woods that excelled in their garden. 'Bon-Bon' was an All-America Rose Selection that even now holds a rating of 7.5. Officially classed as a pink blend, the Woods' bush nevertheless had blossoms that were a solid, intense shade of strawberry pink. The blossoms of its sport were the purest shade of creamy ivory, yet retained the excellent form and size of the parent rose, so we named it 'B'Nilla Bon-Bon.' We were so thrilled with it that I called Dr. Keith Zary at Jackson & Perkins, asking his advice on how to propagate it. He suggested that we send budwood from that branch to him and he would grow and test it for two years to see if it was worthy of being introduced into commerce. In the meantime, I rooted the first bloom, which grew into a big, strong plant. From time to time, however, a cane reverted to its parent 'Bon-Bon.' Alas, at the end of two years, Dr. Zary said that indeed it was a beautiful, striking rose—but that like its parent, it did not grow in the field well enough to make it economically feasible to put into production.

'Bon-Bon' Floribunda (top) and its sport
'B'Nilla Bon-Bon' (bottom)

Several years ago Sean McCann, who loves Floribundas, featured our 'B'Nilla Bon-Bon' in one of his regular articles in *American Rose* magazine. Many growers were intrigued enough with sports to write or call about 'B'Nilla Bon-Bon.' From time to time we've had other sports develop, but nothing as spectacular as this one.

Just this week another surprise occurred that is a first in our garden. There is a small, roofless porch between the house and garden. At daybreak I almost always take my first cup of coffee to that open porch, just to look for overnight developments. The porch is about three feet high, well above the bushes, and affords an excellent overall view. I was standing there, admiring a tall bush heavily laden with early-April buds on which the sepals had fallen. The variety was perfectly evident: 'Classic Touch,' that exquisite, pearl-pink Hybrid Tea of extraordinary form and longevity. Suddenly, I noticed a huge, flaming-orange bud just beginning to unfurl on the same bush! It was right in the

'Touch of Class' and its sport, 'Classic Touch'

center of 'Classic Touch,' with tall major canes all around it, each terminating in huge buds. The bright orange bud was considerably lower on the bush than the others, and I thought: Goody, goody! A sport on 'Classic Touch'! Won't that be grand?

Two days later, the bud fully opened. It was then that I realized that one large cane had reverted to 'Touch of Class,' the parent from which the sport 'Classic Touch' was "born." Closer examination revealed that a major basal, straight and strong and of good color, had put off a lateral about six inches from the bud union. It too was strong and straight and almost as large as the basal from which it had branched. We have never seen a more perfect 'Touch of Class.' The next day several of the other buds opened just as perfectly, all typically 'Classic Touch.'

Only time will tell if this one cane will continue to produce true 'Touch of Class' blooms. If it does, it will be an extraordinary surprise, for these two varieties are the epitome of superb roses.

Not unlike beauty itself…
A rose is in the heart of the beholder.

There is an art in naming roses, a fine-tuned art that is sensitive to the meanings deeper than the surface of the petals. Many times, as almost any reference book on roses will tell you, roses are named for people: family, friends, sweethearts, celebrities. Others are named for their country of origin or for a memorable event. Some hybridizers try to think of names that will be very commercial, very easy to remember, and which will easily be identified with the particular rose being named.

'Dolly Parton' Hybrid Tea, seven inches wide

Dolly Parton, country diva

One of the most notable names among roses ever introduced into commerce is 'Peace' (AARS/1946). Its name commemorates the end of World War II. 'Peace' received the Portland Gold Medal Award in 1944, the ARS National Gold Medal Certificate and the NRS Gold Medal in 1947, and was named "Golden Rose of the Hague" in 1965. It is widely believed that 'Peace' is the most-photographed rose of all time.

Many a name describes a rose perfectly. One example is 'Double Delight.' How could any name be more appropriate for a rose that quite literally is a double delight every day, with every bud and bloom? Each flower is creamy-white at the base of the petals, which higher up are splashed with strawberry-red hues in no particular pattern. It is not unusual for a full-blown rose to be entirely strawberry red, or in cool, cloudy weather for the bloom to be almost entirely creamy-white, with only the slightest touch of pink on the edges of the outer petals. The name also applies to the heady perfume of this 1977 AARS winner, which was awarded the coveted James Alexander Gamble Rose Fragrance Medal in 1986.

'Dolly Parton' is another totally fitting name. The proof is in seeing the rose and then seeing Dolly in person (or even a good photograph of her). This luminous, orange-red, high-centered, velvet rose is nearly always in perfect form and is five to seven inches across; her fragrance rating and classic elegance are deemed extraordinary, which describes 'Dolly Parton' the rose, or the voluptuous lady herself.

It seems only natural that there is an outstanding rose garden at the Dollywood theme park in Pigeon Forge, Tennessee. Of course, 'Dolly' roses are there—however, it may come as a surprise that *all* the roses are 'Dolly Parton' Hybrid Teas. When speaking with Roy Guthry, who planted and tends the garden, he said the entire garden is a memorial to Dolly's departed friends. "The bushes are planted in 12-gallon containers, which I repot with fresh, good soil every four years… All those 'Dolly Parton' roses, it's really somethin' to see! Every bloom is six to seven inches wide." When asked how the bushes winter in Pigeon Forge, he said, "We put all the pots in a cold frame over winter, where they stay 'til April so we can bring 'em all into bloom first thing in the spring when Dollywood opens for the season. When people start coming, they want to see the roses blooming."

Accounts of how 'Cécile Brünner' was named vary somewhat. According to *Modern Roses 9*, the light-pink Polyantha was developed in or near 1894, the year listed for 'Cécile Brünner,' Climber. According to the account I've heard and read most often, the breeder or hybridizer, whose name was Brünner, was engaged to a young woman named Cécile. Before they could be married, she became gravely ill and died. Following her death he named his new rose 'Cécile Brünner,' also called 'Sweetheart Rose.' Thus, Mr. Brünner's sweetheart lives on in the hearts of those who cherish this small-flowered rose. Blossoms grow on an exceptionally large bush that boasts one bloom to a stem, as well as clusters of twelve to fourteen buds and blooms that grow on canes two feet or more in length. Our bush is a good seven feet tall, and six or more wide. The roses are small, about the size of an average-sized Miniature, but that's where the similarity ends. We have grown 'Cécile' on both 'Dr. Huey' and 'Fortuniana' understock and have found that there is no comparison in bush sizes. The 'Fortuniana' bush outgrows 'Dr. Huey' by at least fifty percent. For us, 'Cécile Brünner' also grows very well on her own roots.

'Permanent Wave,' a watermelon-red Floribunda, is ideally named. Her semi-double blooms are made up of wavy, curly petals that highly resemble permanent wave curls.

The rose 'First Light' and its name are exquisitely synonymous with the birth of a new day. Mounds of clear, glowing pink, single blooms over the entire bowl of the bush are reminiscent of early morning, pink clouds at daybreak. Classed as a Shrub Rose, it's a 1998 AARS winner.

'Double Delight' Hybrid Tea

How many rose growers have said over and over, "'Little Darling' is just that"? This soft yellow and salmon-pink blend Floribunda is a true little darling, in the garden or as a cut rose, and is well-endowed with awards. Records do not reveal how the name came about, but with so superb a rose in form, delicious color and longevity, its name could not be more perfect.

Generally, roses which hybridizers name for themselves are those they judge to be the most superb they will ever breed. After a rose has been named, no other rose can be given that name. If, indeed, the breeder develops a superior rose to one that already bears his name, the new cultivar cannot be given the same name. The story goes that in the late 1950s, the famous German breeder Wilhelm Kordes wanted to name his then-new Hybrid Tea—a cream-tipped rose flushed with crimson—for himself, yet he was reluctant to do so, thinking that in the future he might develop an even more superior cultivar. However, he finally decided to gamble and named the rose 'Kordes Perfecta.' Since other forms of a breeder's name may be used in naming subsequent cultivars, 'Kordes Perfecta Superior' came along a few years later.

Another example is that of 'Fred Edmunds.' The coppery-orange Hybrid Tea that bears his name was awarded the Gold Medal of Portland in 1942 and was an AARS winner in 1944. In 1973, Mr. Edmunds named another superior rose for his wife, calling it 'Wini Edmunds.' This striking Hybrid Tea is red with reverse white, and has captured more attention than the rose named for the breeder himself.

More than food and water,
More than soil and sun,
I need your sweet affection
When the day is done.

'Stolen Moment' Miniature, bred by Sean McCann

MINIATURES: THE WORLD OF MARVELOUS LITTLE ROSES
by Sean McCann

Unabashed in his love of roses, Sean McCann's devotion for the world's most honored flower reaches out from his home in County Dublin, Ireland, not only to the United States but to Australia, New Zealand and even to Muse in Glades County, Florida, a place that not more than a handful of people ever heard of.

A national and international rose authority, Sean is a renowned writer in the celebrated British publications Garden News, The Rose, *and* The Journal of the Royal National Rose Society, *as well as* The American Rose *magazine. He has introduced many popular miniature roses on both sides of the Atlantic and is the author of* Miniature Roses: Their Care and Cultivation. *He is Honorable Vice President of the Royal National Rose Society, and is the recipient of numerous prestigious, international awards including the American Rose Society's Gold Honor Medal and the Australian Gold Medal. Mr. McCann is a frequent lecturer and visitor to the United States.*

He is also author of the acclaimed The Rose, An Encyclopedia of North American Roses, Rosarians, and Rose Lore (*Stackpole Books/USA/1993*), *through which our rose paths "crossed" over the ocean! On the phone, as he was relating some of his travails regarding his book, I asked who was writing about growing roses in Florida. "Oh," he replied, "is it different there?" Before our conversation ended, he invited me to write about Florida 'Fortuniana' rootstock roses. When the book was released, he called from Ireland, lamenting the fact that most of my writing had been cut, as had much of his own manuscript. Nevertheless, it is a handsome, comprehensive book on roses and both Sean and I are happy that at least a modicum of information about roses in Florida is included. When invited to write on miniatures for this book, he was assured it would not be cut! Thus his detailed dissertation on miniatures follows with deepest gratitude.*

Seduction is never far away where roses are concerned. I can be intrigued, aroused and tantalized by a rose quicker (almost) than by human contact. This is not a new involvement, a new affair. It began over 30 years ago when a friend sent me six roses. Up to that time I had no interest whatsoever in gardening, plants or nature. But in no time at all it seemed that the roses took hold of me.

First there were the hybrid teas; then climbers and floribundas. I grew them, exhibited them and finally I began breeding them in a small glass house (12 ft. x 12 ft.).

I began with big roses but one day a little touch of magic invaded my life and the miniatures arrived. Almost immediately I began hybridizing them. This seemed a world apart but as I was now established as a rose writer I reckoned that I should learn as much as I could about every aspect of rose culture.

Since then I have bred many, many miniature roses. Some 30 of them are available in the United States through Jerry Justice in Portland, Oregon. They have not made a fortune for either of us but they have given me great satisfaction—especially when I get a note of appreciation from someone telling me how lovely a particular miniature is. There is also pleasure to hear that one has been awarded a prize at a show somewhere. Among these show winners are 'Swansong,' 'Crazy Dottie' and in recent times my own absolute favorite, 'Stolen Moment.'

For me the miniature rose is one of the most adaptable plants you will ever find. You can put it in a rockery, in a border, in a bed, in a pot; plant it in a window box to brighten a property, or in a tub on top of a high-rise apartment block; grow it in a garden, a greenhouse or a small conservatory; you can even use it as a house plant for long periods of the year. It grows as a small bush or as a ground-cover plant, a hanging plant, or a climber. It comes in every color and mixture of colors that you can ask for—lavenders and greens, whites and yellows, reds and pinks and bicolors as bright as sunshine.

In the past decade, miniature roses have come on so fast that in some parts of the world today more are sold than all other types of roses combined. One Danish firm produces a million small plants a week; in Britain, the Royal National Rose Society has seen the entries of miniatures for its shows increase thirty times; in national shows in the USA the miniature entries often outstrip all others. Yet twenty years ago, miniatures were regarded by many as mere novelty plants. One writer even disparagingly called them "toy roses." What a change he would see today.

While the real popularity of miniatures is of recent development, these little plants were being sold in European markets over a century ago; then they were window ledge plants, sold to be grown in pots and later discarded. But they have come a long way since then.

Where they really began is a secret known only by nature. There is some evidence of miniature roses being sold in Asia and Europe around the 1700s; they probably were developed through various Chinese roses. The origins of the first miniature roses as we know them today are uncertain. The progenitor of practically all the modern miniatures is a rose-red variety called *Rosa rouletii* named to honour a Colonel Roulet, who is said to have spotted its potential when he saw it in a Swiss village at the start of this century. This little rose was then being sold locally as a pot plant, and its commercial introduction on a much wider scale set the miniatures moving. But not all that fast: in the early 1930s there were only four well-known miniatures generally available—*R. rouletii*, *R. indica pumila*, 'Pompon de Paris' and 'Oakington Ruby.' The strange thing about all these is that they are very much alike and you really need to sit down and study the plants to find the differences. But, after careful examination, you will probably find as I did that 'Pompon de Paris' and *R. indica pumila* are one and the same variety; *R. rouletii* resembles

them too, but its blooms tend to be slightly smaller. These three are in similar deep rose to lavender colours, depending on where and how they are grown. 'Oakington Ruby,' which is named for the village where it was bred in Cambridge, England, is red with a slight touch of white in the centre of the bloom.

'Rise 'n' Shine' Miniature

There were people who saw the opportunities in the miniatures and they set about breeding new varieties using the original four as parents. The real breakthrough came with the arrival in 1935, from a Dutchman, Jan de Vink, of the crimson 'Peon,' appropriately renamed 'Tom Thumb' by Robert Pyle when he introduced it to the United States. Pyle introduced a number of other varieties, as did Thomas Robinson in England and the Spanish hybridist, Pedro Dot, who had a string of successes that included the perfect little white 'Pour Toi' (also known as 'For You,' 'Para Ti' and 'Wendy').

Then came the creations of Ralph S. Moore, a rose breeder in Visalia in central California. He is the father of the modern miniature and his many varieties have swept through the world of roses. He continues to strengthen his string, giving us miniature roses in every conceivable colour, shape and size: varieties such as 'Rise 'n' Shine' (yellow), 'Magic Carousel' (red and white), 'Easter Morning' (creamy white), 'Little Buckaroo' (red), 'Baby Darling' (salmon-orange), 'Beauty Secret' (red), 'Earthquake' (red and yellow stripes), 'Lavender Lace' (mauve-lavender), 'Over the Rainbow' (red and yellow)—and a whole host named for friends and famous people of the rose world.

He cannot put a finger on the time when, in his home town (he has hardly ever left Visalia, California, for any length of time except to get his degree at Davis University in Sacramento) he began to work with miniatures. But in his early twenties he decided to touch a rainbow. He began collecting hips from roses around his home and found himself growing small plants from the seeds. One of the roses he was using for seeds was the lovely little 'Cécile Brünner,' a hybrid polyantha, with very small and beautiful blooms; this was the rose that gave him a lifelong love of tiny roses.

The roses he produced were small, healthy and in a mass of colors that had never been seen before; in fact his small roses were far in advance of anything that had ever been done with the miniatures. Today these early miniatures will be found in the breeding lines of practically every miniature in the world.

Other rose breeders have not been backward in praising the work of this pioneer. New Zealand's Sam McGredy once wrote: "Whenever I think of miniatures I immediately think of Ralph Moore. No-one else has done so much to improve the type and to make them popular… He had the vision and he was dreaming his dreams of minis when none of the rest of us bothered."

How do you build a new line of roses? Not just through dreaming—Ralph Moore gave his own explanation. "It is like engineering—you've got to see the finished concept in its entirety. When Joseph Baermann Strauss designed the Golden Gate Bridge he saw that bridge complete before anything was in place. Nobody else did—but he saw the whole thing—that's what a hybridizer has to do. You've got to dream for your ruffled rose, for your climber and learn how to engineer your way to it, whether it takes two years, ten years or twenty years. It's a mental thing first… something way beyond today…"

Other top rose breeders decided that they could not be left out of the action. Famous names such as McGredy (New Zealand), Kordes (Germany), Poulsen (Denmark), Dickson (Ireland) and a great flurry of hybridists in the USA—Saville, Jolly, Dee

Bennett, Ernest Williams, Ben Williams, Dennis and Suzy Bridges, Michael and Betty Williams, Laurie Chaffin, Pete and Kay Taylor and many others have offered new roses in the miniature style.

What is miniature style? To many people, a miniature rose is a small bush with small blooms but it has gone way beyond this concept. Today you can get the miniature rose growing on shrub-like bushes, there is a whole range of climbing miniatures, there is a slightly larger range called "patio roses" in Europe (these grow with larger blooms and on larger plants) and of course there are those that grow as little mounds of blooms to cover awkward spots in the garden landscape—tumbling over walls and down banks, or growing under the feet of other roses, thus cutting out the problem of weeding.

The real boom, though, is and will continue to be in "true" miniatures, little roses on little bushes that will grow anywhere, bringing their own beauty to places where roses could never be grown before. Children can have them in their own tiny gardens; they can bring great pleasure to the handicapped, who can work with them on a bench or a table. They are easy to manage, and as easy to propagate as geraniums—and are so much smaller than the accepted garden roses, in fact you could say that they are half the size with twice the appeal.

Taking care of miniatures is simplicity itself. The simple formula is as good for humans as it is for roses—give them air, sun, water, food and a little bit of love.

If you put all these aspects together you will discover that they are all taken care of under the one heading—love. If you love them you will make sure they have air around them to stop diseases taking over; they will have sun for at least six hours a day (but less will do); they will have water so that the roots do not dry out. They need more than a little dribble here and there that will just wet the top soil. You must give your roses a good, deep watering that gets right to the roots.

There are many ways to make sure your roses are correctly watered, ranging from elaborate automatic systems to the good old watering can. If you can afford a built-in watering system with an auto-

'Minnie Pearl' Miniature

too closely to this half strength formula—not only do they halve the amount of fertiliser but they double the time between feedings. That is a diet on which many miniatures perish.

Everyone has their own idea of what a rose fertiliser should be—there are enough to pick from and most of them will do the right job for your miniatures—and other roses too. There are many different formulations on the market so select carefully. Some are more suitable for tomatoes than roses as the nitrogen content is almost fatally high. Soluble fertilisers have their place as well and will provide a quicker return from your roses than nature intends. Applied to the root zone it can work its own wonders.

Taking care in this simple way of your miniatures means that you should never have to say sorry to them.

matic timer, your workload will certainly be lessened but you will miss a lot from not visiting each bush regularly. Watering by hand, whether it is from a hose or a can, does give you the opportunity to make sure that nothing unusual is happening to your bushes. A good water wand or hose attachment will be of great benefit in taking the pressure off your back but still allowing you to get around to see what is happening on the ground.

Miniatures in containers need far more care than those in the ground, and the smaller the pot the quicker it will dry out. If a pot does dry out it should be left standing in water for several hours to recover.

Feeding often causes problems for growers. Don't overfeed and don't starve them. An extra "little spoonful just for luck" will cause more problems than anything else. Much more harm is done to roses by over fertilising than by under fertilising but under fertilising causes problems when gardeners take to the theory that being half-sized roses they only need half feeding. Many gardeners stick

The Top Miniatures

The American Rose Society poll of the top ten miniatures for exhibition shows that a great collection would also be reliable as general garden or container grown varieties:

'Fairhope'	'Jean Kenneally'
'Irresistible'	'Snow Bride'
'Hot Tamale'	'Pierrine'
'Kristin'	'Incognito'
'Minnie Pearl'	'Luis Desamero'

Older varieties tend to fade away but are still prominent in gardens where they have shown their ability to become established. This list would include (in my view):

'Rise 'n' Shine'	'Cinderella'
'June Laver'	'Beauty Secret'
'Black Jade'	'Lady in Red'
'Party Girl'	'Jennifer'
'Little Jackie'	'Rose Gilardi'
'Rainbow's End'	'Little Artist'
'Gourmet Popcorn'	'Cuddles'

Although endowed with a little face,
Up from a secret hiding place
The little rose rises and blooms with grace.

ULTIMATE EASY ROSES

by Dr. Malcolm Manners

Dr. Manners is Professor of Citrus and Environmental Horticulture at Florida Southern College in Lakeland, Florida. The following is reprinted with his permission, from the October 1994 issue of The Cherokee Rose.

"One comes back to those old-fashioned roses as one does to old music and poetry. A garden needs old associations, old fragrances, as a home needs things that have been lived with."
— *The Rose Annual,* 1928

For more than a year, I've been thinking about writing an article on the most carefree roses in our gardens. This seems like a good time to do so. While there are many roses that grow and even thrive with relatively little care, there are only a few with such cast-iron constitutions that they are truly carefree in our climate. I've chosen eight favorites to describe.

'Louis Philippe' (a.k.a. the "Cracker Rose"): If I had to pick a most carefree-of-all-roses, this would be it. A rather slow-growing bush, but eventually reaches huge sizes. I've seen them around ten feet tall and at least that wide, but those were ancient bushes. They do live to great ages, even here in Central Florida and on their own roots. The flowers are one to three inches across, solid red in some weather, or otherwise red with a large pinkish-white center. Slightly fragrant. I see more old plants of 'Louis Philippe' in this area than any other rose. It makes an outstanding clipped hedge (or if you have acres, an unclipped hedge!), or a large specimen plant.

'Old Blush': Nearly as problem-free as 'Louis Philippe.' 'Old Blush' can also reach large size, but not as big as 'Louis.' Its flowers open light to medium-pink, and darken to deep pink or light red in the sun. This is another good hedge rose, and has been used in that way across our campus. Clip it with a hedge trimmer, mowing it off to the desired height and width—it doesn't care what you do to it. Also thrives on its own roots. Against a wall, it may show a little powdery mildew in the late winter, but not enough to worry about.

R. laevigata (a.k.a. the 'Cherokee Rose'): This is a great tree-climbing rose, in that it is a massive climber which will outgrow most trellises or arbors. It is once-blooming, but the bloom season is quite long, often beginning in November and continuing through April. The plant is quite disease-free and thrives on its own roots. It is viciously thorny. Big three-inch-plus, pure white, single flowers, with bright yellow stamens in the middle.

'Mrs. B. R. Cant': Tea roses are noted for becoming large bushes, but 'Mrs. B. R. Cant' is a giant even among the Teas. Mine are planted six to seven feet from their neighbors. If I were doing it over, I'd put them ten feet apart, and even then they would touch each other within a couple years. 'Mrs. B. R. Cant' makes big, three- to five-inch very double, deep pink-to-red flowers with a nice tea scent. It is highly disease-resistant, and is acceptable on its own roots if you plant it near a building or other concrete slab. Otherwise, I'd recommend that it be grafted to 'Fortuniana' roots. We have one of these on our campus known to be over 30 years old, which gets no water, fertilizer, sprays, or "correct" pruning. Yet it thrives and blooms nearly constantly.

'Tausendschön': I found this rose growing in a lime-rock parking lot at a local transmission shop. The proprietor's wife said it had been given to her at least ten years earlier as a cutting. She had done nothing to it at all, once she planted it in the parking lot. She gave me cuttings, and we now grow it on the campus. This rose is highly blackspot resistant but does get some powdery mildew in cool weather. It has a long bloom season in the spring, then a few flowers here and there throughout the summer, then rather good bloom again in the fall. It makes a very large bush or a moderate climber. We grow it as a climber. In addition to being carefree, it is nearly thornless, so is pleasant to work with. It makes big clusters of small, medium-pink flowers.

R. rugosa rubra: Rugosa roses aren't supposed to grow well in the hot South, but I learned from Dr. Robert Basye, in Texas, that it is their roots, not their tops, which resent the heat. Grafted or budded on 'Fortuniana,' this rose becomes completely carefree. It gets no diseases at all, blooms nearly constantly, and is a tight, compact bush. Flowers are medium large, two to three inches, single, bright purplish-pink. I would assume that other forms of this species might do as well, but I have not tried them.

'Spray Cécile Brünner' (a.k.a. 'Bloomfield Abundance,' the "Sweetheart Rose"): This is another very large-growing plant, making a massive bush. It blooms nearly constantly, with huge sprays of tiny flesh-pink flowers. Grows well on its own roots, even in the Miami area. It blackspots badly in October, but is disease-free the rest of the year. So, we just consider it a deciduous rose, and don't worry about it.

'Pink Pet' (a.k.a. 'Caldwell Pink,' mainly in Texas): A favorite for hedges, this rose can grow to be eight or more feet tall, or can be clipped to stay short and tidy. It constantly produces big clusters of small, very double, bright pink flowers. The leaves appear to be completely immune to blackspot. It does get some powdery mildew in the winter. Control it by pruning the affected limbs off. This is another rose that we prune with a hedge trimmer, with no ill effects. Excellent on its own roots or grafted.

Others: There are undoubtedly other roses that would also thrive on neglect, but I haven't had enough experience to recommend them for such conditions. For example, I suspect that some of the Bermuda roses would be good "survivors," especially 'Smith's Parish,' which seems to be completely disease-free for us. I don't generally recommend roses for a completely untended garden. Any rose, including those listed here, will certainly respond to good care, particularly adequate irrigation and fertilization. But in a situation where one can't give consistent, proper care, these varieties will perform quite adequately anyway. And even if you fuss constantly with your roses, to produce the "perfect" garden, these varieties will grow and bloom beautifully for you. I highly recommend them.

On wings of morning a silent prayer,
For fragrance of roses floating on air...
On wings of morning... an answered prayer.

DAVID AUSTIN ROSES YOU CAN LIVE WITH

By Jim Small, ARS Consulting Rosarian, Central Florida Rose Society

The Modern Shrub roses hybridized by David Austin have become increasingly popular in recent years. Produced from crosses of Gallicas, Damasks and other Old Garden Roses with Hybrid Teas, Floribundas, and Climbers, they combine the character, form, fragrance, and growth habit of the old roses with the repeat flowering habit and color range of modern forms. David Austin has christened the more than 80 varieties produced since the early 1960s the "English Roses" and considers them a new class. Both the American Rose Society and the World Federation of Rose Societies, however, do not recognize this classification and place the Austin roses among the Shrubs.

Like many other rosarians, I have become enamored with the old-fashioned charm and fragrance of the Austin roses. As much as I love my Hybrid Tea roses for their beautiful form and predictable growth habit, they do not produce the sensory impact of my Shrub and Old Garden Roses. Visitors to my garden are naturally drawn by the overpowering fragrance and end up spending most of their time among the old roses and Shrubs, marveling at their beauty.

Now that I have told you how much I like many of the Austin roses, I must admit that, despite their considerable charm, they do have many weaknesses. Indeed, one judge recently told me that he was digging them all up as he had never found one that was any good. While I vehemently disagreed with his statement, I had to admit that there were problems with many varieties and that I could recommend only a few. These problems include the variable growth form of many varieties, the lack of hardiness in some, and the poor frequency of blooming of several forms in our area. Many grow to a very large size, making them unsuitable for smaller gardens. Recently, I measured diameters of 9–11 feet and heights up to 12 feet for 'Mary Rose,' 'Abraham Darby,' 'Swan,' 'Fisherman's Friend' and 'L. D. Braithwaite' in a friend's garden. Varieties like 'Graham Thomas,' 'The Herbalist,' and 'Symphony' bloom sparsely or infrequently in our Florida climate. It is also difficult to know about the growth habits of Austin roses before you buy them as most guides and catalogs give growth information from England. It is the experience of most American rosarians that the English Roses grow considerably larger here. I recently ordered some Austin roses that were listed as being of small stature but quickly found them to be monsters in my garden, overtaking the space occupied by other roses. Although the *Arena Rose Catalog* gives estimates of the ultimate size of these varieties in the United States (really California), I have found that several forms exceed their values in Florida.

In order to help those of you who are thinking about adding Austin Roses to your garden and have limited space, I have prepared the following short descriptions of the varieties that I find to be most suitable. If you have the space (12-foot diameter), roses like 'Heritage,' 'Abraham Darby,' 'L. D. Braithwaite' and others can be wonderful additions to your garden. I don't have that kind of space, so my criteria for "Austin Roses you can live with" are that the growth form be reasonably upright (as opposed to sprawling), that the diameter occupied be no greater than four feet, the height no greater than six feet, and that the bloom be prolific and reasonably frequent. If you can obtain the variety on 'Fortuniana' rootstock, that is a plus to be considered. Here then are the top varieties of Austin Roses that "you can live with."

'ENGLISH GARDEN': This rose may be the best performer of all the English Roses I grow. The color is a buff yellow to beige, depending on the weather. It is a prolific bloomer with large, flat flowers composed of many tiny petals. The bush is very upright with a diameter of about three feet and a height of four. In my garden it has been relatively disease free. The only disparagement I can give it is that, to my nose, it is not particularly fragrant. The slight fragrance reminds one of the Tea roses.

'FAIR BIANCA': A creamy white rose of unusual beauty with a strong myrrh fragrance. The flowers are in the form of a shallow cup packed with petals. The bush grows upright with a diameter of about 3 feet and a height of 4.5 feet. Sometimes there are so many blooms on a cane that it droops to the ground. Overall, this is a wonderful rose that deserves a place in every garden. It may take a while to get started but it is worth the wait. It also is readily available on 'Fortuniana.' This rose was named for Bianca, the sister of Katharina in Shakespeare's *Taming of the Shrew.*

'AMBRIDGE ROSE': This rose is one of my newest additions and already a favorite. The cupped blossoms are a warm apricot to pink with a most pleasant fragrance. It is a good bloomer, producing only a few less flowers than the preceding varieties. In my garden it is three feet in diameter and slightly less than four feet tall. The rose was named after a British radio and TV serial, *The Archers.*

'THE WIFE OF BATH': A rose with flowers of silvery pink on a twiggy but upright shrub. In my garden the bush is 3 feet in diameter and 5.5 feet tall. It blooms prolifically and has a strong fragrance of myrrh. It is hardy but requires some pruning of the twiggy canes. This rose, named after the character in Chaucer's great work, will make an excellent addition to your garden.

'BELLE STORY': A fragrant, semi-double rose with large blossoms that curve inward toward the bright yellow stamens. The color is a delicate shade of pink. My bush is about 3 feet in diameter and about 5.5 feet tall. It is an excellent performer in the garden. The name commemorates the first woman to serve in the Royal Navy as a nursing sister in the 1880s. I am also growing 'South Moon,' a white sport of 'Belle Story' which has most of the good characteristics of the parent.

'TAMORA': Another recent addition to my garden and is already a favorite. It is an extremely prolific bloomer with apricot pink flowers. The fragrance reminds one of myrrh. My bush is about three feet in diameter and less than five feet tall. David Austin calls it "a nice little rose that has been largely superseded by 'Jayne Austin' and 'Sweet Juliet.'" I could not disagree more. In my garden, 'Sweet Juliet' turned out to be a stingy bloomer with a sprawling growth pattern. I am definitely not listing it as "a rose you can live with." Indeed, it has recently been "shovel pruned." 'Tamora' is by far the better rose in my opinion.

'THE PRINCE': A crimson rose that becomes closer to purple as it ages. It is supposed to have a low spreading growth form but my bush, grafted on 'Fortuniana,' is upright. The diameter is slightly less than three feet and the height about five feet. It has a very strong, old-rose fragrance and blooms frequently. My bush seems hardy and grows well but I would recommend that you give it a little more fertilizer than the others. In hot weather the petals may burn.

'GLAMIS CASTLE': Another recent addition that shows much promise. The flowers are pure white, with old-fashioned form and strong fragrance. The bush is a slow grower but it blooms prolifically. This shrub grows to about four feet with a diameter of about three feet. The growth form is upright and compact. The rose is named after the famous Scottish castle that was the Queen Mother's ancestral home.

'ST. CECELIA': This rose is listed by the American Rose Society as medium yellow, but the blossoms are really a shade of pink fading to almost white. It blooms well (but not as prolifically as 'Glamis Castle') and has a strong myrrh fragrance. It has a diameter of three feet and reaches a height of about five feet.

'PRETTY JESSICA': This is a wonderful little rose with bright pink flowers and a sweet fragrance. It grows to a diameter of three feet and reaches a height of less than four feet. It is a slow grower but blooms prolifically. Of all the roses mentioned above, it probably takes up the least space.

'THE SQUIRE': This rose lies at the end of the spectrum of smaller Austin Shrubs. The blooms are large and bright red, with a strong fragrance. The bush itself grows to heights to six feet or more and the diameter is over four feet. For the most part, the growth is upright. I really like this rose but you will need to give it more space than the others.

There you have it. The best Austin roses. Plant them on five-foot centers in good rich soil, spray them, give them plenty of water, sunshine, and a fraction of the fertilizer that you give your Hybrid Teas and you will be well rewarded with an abundance of fragrant flowers with an old-fashioned charm.

The American Rose Society produces an annual handbook for selecting roses, a guide to aid in finding roses in which you might be interested, titled *Handbook for Selecting Roses and ARS Exhibition Names*.

With the exception of the 2000 issue, in which the roses are listed by classification, the roses are listed alphabetically. (For the first time, the 2000 *Handbook* listed roses by classification rather than alphabetically by name. There was such overwhelming objection to this method that for the 2001 *Handbook*, the ARS went back to the original alphabetical listing, which enables the finding of any rose, regardless of whether its classification is known. This is a fine example of the wisdom in the old line "Let the people be heard"—especially rose growers!) The name of each rose is followed by its classification, color class and rating as compiled from members of the ARS through their Roses in Review and Triennial Survey programs.

Many among us mistakenly think this rating guide is primarily for those who grow "show" roses—that is, roses to be entered in competition in shows. However, the little book is far more. The numbers 1 through 10 are an indication of compiled performance records of roses all over the country—in various climates, conditions, with good care and not-so-good care, et cetera.

In the book itself the note is made that if a cultivar's rating is less than 6, the rose is probably of questionable value. However, the ratings are not to be taken as gospel, but are more of a guide.

For instance, 'Color Magic' is a rose of rare, true beauty—in size, form, and coloring, as its countless awards will attest. I envy those who grow this rose successfully. Alas, we are not among them. We've lost count of the 'Color Magic' bushes we've planted. Each has done well for several months, producing large, extraordinary blooms. Then, sooner than later, each bush has gone into a decline

'Color Magic' Hybrid Tea

that we've been unable to reverse. Thus, as of this writing, our garden is without 'Color Magic'—not a pleasant fact to admit. Neighbor Lynn Woods has had similar experiences with this cultivar, yet I must confess, she's done better with it than we have. However, we both agree: 'Color Magic' is one of those "we can't live without." Nationwide, its rating in both 1997 and 1998 is 8.2, yet there are those of us in South Florida who, in all honesty, could not rate it more than a 7.0, considering its lack of strength and vigor. From the standpoint of exceptional beauty, color, form and size, we could easily give it a 9.0 plus rating.

According to the 1997 *Handbook*: "Some roses perform better in specific geographical areas than in others. For example, the 'Shreveport' rose, named for the American Rose Society's headquarters city, grows magnificently in Shreveport. It is a healthy plant with an abundance of color all year. We would rate it an 8.5 or 9.0. Nationwide, however, it carries a 6.7 rating, indicating only fair performance."

The kernel of truth is there's no practical explanation as to why some bushes excel for some of us in our respective locations, while others do not. This, of course, assumes that various plants receive more or less the same care and attention. At any rate, it is disappointing and disheartening. If there is a tried and true answer as to why this happens and what to do about it, I do not know where to find it. If the cultivar we've lost in such a manner is a real favorite, we try to find another bush, ideally from a different grower or company, in the hope that perhaps the lost bush was an inferior one and the same cultivar from a different grower or source might be stronger.

Grandpa once said, "Well, it may be a little like children. Some of 'em get a cold and seem to be sickly real often, catchin' ever'thing that comes along—and some of 'em never do."

His favorite rose was the old 'American Beauty,' which at one time was said to be the most widely grown variety in the world. It was indeed the most widely grown in my growing-up world in Virginia, because my mother planted one rooted from a cutting of my grand-mother's bush at the east end of our porch, and forever after she kept rooting them until they grew like walls around that porch.

It's interesting to note that this old rose, listed as a Hybrid Perpetual, still carries a 7.5 rating while the 'American Beauty' Climber, listed as a Large Flowered Climber, is rated at only 6.3. 'American Beauty,' which has always been thought of as a red rose, is designated by the ARS as deep pink. (This rose should not be confused with 'Miss All-American Beauty,' a Hybrid Tea, whose color is also listed as deep pink. 'Miss All-American Beauty' won the coveted AARS award in 1968.)

When it comes to Roses, some of us are incurable.
Eleanor Perenyi

It was reported many years ago that 60 percent of all roses sold in the florist trade were 'Better Times' (1934). Described as a very vigorous rose, medium red with dark, leathery foliage, 'Better Times' is a Hybrid Tea sport of 'Briarcliff' (1926), which in turn was a sport of 'Columbia' (1916). Today, 'Better Times' is difficult to find. Once in a while I've run across a plant in a roadside nursery, but not often.

Ratings do change from year to year, but rarely is the change more than plus or minus one point. This is because a different set of growers enter their findings each year, and because some growers may alter their assessment of respective roses over time.

The small ARS rating handbook (pocket size) is published by and available from the American Rose Society, contact information for which is listed in the "Sources for Roses and Supplies" list at the end of this book.

The roses long to see you, all of them… and so do I.

ROSES–THEIR GIFT OF FRAGRANCE

According to Greek mythology, the goddess of flowers, Chloris, created the rose. It happened this way: One day in the woods, she found the body of a lifeless nymph and immediately turned her into a flower. However, not being exactly satisfied with what she had done, she called upon Aphrodite, goddess of love, and Dionysus, god of wine, to enhance the flower, which they did exquisitely. Aphrodite bestowed beauty upon the flower and Dionysus added nectar to give it a sweet scent. Zephyr, the West Wind, got busy and blew away all the clouds so Apollo, the sun god, could shine and make it blossom forth in spectacular beauty.

Having so amply blessed the rose, all the gods gathered together and decided that something very special had to take place. Their unanimous decision was to crown the rose the "Queen of Flowers." And so, even unto this day, the title has not only remained but has grown in status and stature.

Down through the centuries drifts the pure, sweet fragrance of roses: some subtle, even slight, some heavy, almost overpowering. When we smell a fragrant rose, we experience a remarkable sensation, one that brings the outside world into the body through our senses. Information is transmitted to the brain, which selects, organizes and interprets it, in a process we call perception.

'Ave Maria' Hybrid Tea

The aroma produced by an essential oil has three recognizable constituents. The "top" constituents are the light and "fresh" notes, those with a sweet or delicate odor. They are the first to be absorbed by the olfactory organs, but are the least persistent. The "middle" constituents are the main ingredients of the aroma and provide the sustained notes. The "base" constituents are rich and heavy in character. They are the last aromas to reach the nose and provide a scent's staying power.

Not too many years ago, if a rose had a scent, it was all the better. If it was scentless, it did not make a lot of difference; if it was pretty, that was enough. Not so today. Fragrance—heavy fragrance—is much in demand and becoming more so all the time. Many hybridizers try to breed fragrance into their new cultivars, just as they do color and form. And oh, how successful they've been!

The James Alexander Gamble Rose Fragrance Medal honors outstanding cultivars specifically for their scent. Among those which have received the medal are 'Crimson Glory' (1961), 'Chrysler Imperial' (1965), 'Fragrant Cloud' (1969), and 'Double Delight' (1986).

In no particular order, some of those that we have grown that are at the head of the perfume class include 'Angel Face,' 'Dolly Parton,' and 'Tropicana.' It is a mystery why these three did not win the coveted Gamble award. Without fail, in any season, these roses draw attention with their extraordinary perfume. Others commanding just as much notice include 'Perfume Delight,' 'Secret,' 'Don Juan,' 'Ave Maria,' 'Miss All-American

'Perfume Delight' Hybrid Tea

Beauty,' 'Bob Hope,' 'Sterling Silver,' 'Fragrant Hour,' 'Konrad Adenauer,' 'Eiffel Tower,' 'Editor McFarland,' 'Rubaiyat,' 'Royal Highness,' 'Elizabeth of Glamis,' 'Kordes Perfecta,' 'Love Song' and many more.

Although our garden never "sleeps," the fragrance intensity of roses does vary considerably with the changing seasons. When summer is hot and high the roses will be less fragrant, especially during a dry spell. Yet even in summer, in the early morning hours, as well as just before dark, the level of perfume is greatly enhanced.

The fragrance of roses means far more than just sweet scents to lift the spirits and delight those who tend them. Their perfume brings a nostalgia, a euphoria that can be felt only by close and gentle association. The language of roses is worth listening for.

The sweet, pure innocence of roses…
Their scent reaches out to touch us.

Sweet-smelling Climber 'Don Juan'

Dr. James Alexander Gamble

For a rose to receive the James Alexander Gamble Rose Fragrance Medal is an outstanding achievement. While some awards are no doubt made for "political" reasons, such cannot be said of this one. The proof is in burying the nose in the rose and inhaling! Which is not to say that every magnificently fragrant rose has won the medal. This could not be. However, many of the most deliciously fragrant roses are the recipients of this prestigious and coveted award, all due to the devoted, dedicated work of the rosarian who spent most of his life in pursuit of the fragrance of roses, Dr. James Gamble.

As a young boy, Bob Grant of Archer, Florida not only worked for Dr. Gamble, he studied with him for years, learning first hand about the intricacies of fragrance in roses. Here, Bob Grant relates some of his experiences with the rosarian to whom the world of fragrant roses owes so much.

"Dr. James Gamble was a neighbor at Tall Timbers in Southern Maryland where I lived. This area, located on the banks of the lower Potomac River, has a mild microclimate due to the warm salt waters of the river. It was a great area for growing many kinds of plants, including roses. My family always had a large rose garden so I had the privilege of experiencing the beauty of many heirloom roses.

"Because of my interest in roses, at the young age of eight years I would spend many hours with a fellow rosarian, James Gamble. Dr. Gamble was a quiet, studious, energetic man. In his retirement years, he was completely devoted to growing and promoting fragrant Hybrid Tea roses.

"In the 1940s, he carved his rose garden out of the pinewoods in Tall Timbers. This was no easy task, as the loblolly pines were of large diameter and at least 80 feet in height. A crew of local farmers removed all the stumps and roots by hand.

"Dr. Gamble's goal was to build a reference collection of climbing Hybrid Tea roses. He considered the climbing Hybrid Tea cultivars to be even more beautiful than their bush counterparts. He loved their long stems and massive flowers with their outstanding fragrances. I can remember, as a kid, watching him take one of these huge individual blooms in both hands and bury his nose among the petals to absorb the wonderful aroma. He would remove his nose from the bloom and let out a contented snort. As he described the aroma, he would let me sample the fragrance, and then he'd talk about the rose's lineage. He could usually tell where in a rose's lineage that particular fragrance came from.

"Most of his winter months were spent poring over books and documents to chart the ancestry of fragrant roses. This was a time before computers and so all of his work was done by hand with chart after chart stacked on a large table. I would spend many hours listening to him describe the history of the older roses with their wondrous fragrances.

"Starting in my pre-teen years, I maintained the garden for Dr. Gamble. The large plants were grown upright and then trained on many lines of wire, forming trellises. I remember quite vividly the large piston-type sprayer that was so difficult to move. You can name your poison, and we used it for insects and disease prevention. I used to become covered with all of it! This was before any concern for chemicals affecting humans or the environment. Needless to say, after spraying, I would rush home and take a long shower!

"The garden was very beautiful, especially in the late spring. The climbers would be covered with large blooms of many subtle colors. After I went to college to study horticulture, I lost touch with Dr. Gamble and his rose garden. When I visited Tall Timbers in later years, the garden was all gone. A house stood on the site. I only hope that the garden material was moved to a suitable location and not just ploughed under.

"Jim Gamble wrote and published a special little book that is a delight to read (*Roses Unlimited*). It included an excellent section on rose fragrance. I especially enjoyed reading the history of the older Hybrid Teas such as 'Madame Butterfly,' 'Ophelia,' 'Lady Mary Fitzwilliam,' 'La France' and 'Radiance.' Unfortunately, I have lost my signed copy. I would so enjoy reading it again from cover to cover."

Roses leave fragrance in the hand of those that bestow them.
— Chinese proverb

Regardless of rootstock, the importance of a strong, healthy bush cannot be overstated. A weak, sickly plant will likely remain weak and sickly, and a misshapen bush isn't desirable either. You can save yourself a lot of trouble by inspecting all plants thoroughly before buying them. First, look at the graft. It should be reasonably smooth, without cracks, holes, or twists. Master (basal) canes should grow from all sides of it, as opposed to one or two canes emerging from just one side. A bad graft will never right itself into becoming a good, productive one.

Next, look at the size and color of the canes. They should be a strong, healthy green (never yellowish), without cracks or breaks, preferably at least $3/8$ of an inch in diameter. The overall shape of the bush is also important. Choose bushes with major canes that are more or less evenly spaced and that grow upward and outward. Careful pruning can improve the shape of some bushes, but a bush with many canes that touch or cross, or one that is particularly one-sided is usually not a desirable bush. Leave it to become a challenge for someone else!

The condition of leaves communicates a lot about the overall condition of the plant. Inspect the foliage carefully. If it is not vibrant green, free of insects and diseases (blackspot, mildew, etc.), don't buy the plant! You'll be doing yourself a favor simply to walk away from such a rose. Not only will it be a continual disappointment, but you'll be buying problems and taking them home to infect other plants. For instance, one plant badly infested with red spider mites can infest a whole rose garden in 24 hours! Red spider mites are all but impossible to see with the naked eye, but their damage to rose foliage is unmistakable. These tiny mites feed on the soft, tender tissue of the undersides of leaves, causing them to turn dry, brittle, and reddish-brown, after which they quickly slough from the plant. Red spider mites may infest your roses sooner or later but the last thing you want to do is to buy a batch and take them home!

If a rosebush appears to be old, or if it has a huge, bulbous graft or cracked bark on the trunk or canes, leave it for someone else. It will take the same amount of time, energy and ingredients to plant an old, worn-out or sick bush as it will to plant a young, healthy bush that promises years of productivity ahead.

Of course, if you find a variety you "can't live without" that you've been unable to find elsewhere, go ahead and buy it, even if it's not a number one plant. But decide right then and there to isolate that bush until you're sure it has no disease nor insects that will infest your other bushes. We did this very thing with 'Natalie.' We had called or visited every grower we knew of with no luck, so when we noticed a plant in a small garden center not known for good roses, we bought it—even though it was covered with blackspot, had only a few spindly canes, and was without a label. The garden center owner had no idea of its identity. Although its one bloom was small, misshapen and wilted, there was no mistaking that color! We wondered if it would live until we got it home. It appeared so weak we doubted it could survive planting until we could improve its condition. Thinking it might have problems less evident than blackspot and spider mites, we kept it away from the garden for weeks. Finally, it started to recover, putting out new growth on old canes and producing one small new basal. Then and only then did we plant it in the garden.

Now, a year or so later, it still has not become a big, vigorous plant, but it has recovered remarkably and blooms admirably, particularly considering its inauspicious beginning. In the 1998 *Handbook for Selecting Roses*, 'Natalie' is listed as a medium-pink Floribunda, but wherever I have seen her, her color is an intense coral-pink. 'Natalie' has an 8.0 rating. As a cut rose, this one rivals the lasting qualities of 'Don Juan' and 'St. Patrick.'

Now that you have come to the garden, I can smile again.

2. Site Selection and Planning

GEOGRAPHY AND ROSES

Those new to growing roses often ask: What's different about growing roses in different parts of the country—or even in different parts of one state—for example, south Florida to north Florida?

The short answer is that the art, the exercise, of growing roses is relatively the same everywhere after the roses are planted. Even the planting technique—actually putting the bush in the ground—varies more with the individual rose grower than it does with geography. While some growers go "all out" when planting a bush, using a number of different soil amendments at planting time, others prefer using just the basics: about a third humus/compost, peat and existing soil, plus manure in some form. Most growers use a soil mixture somewhere in between, regardless of where they live. For instance, when we grew roses in Virginia and the Carolinas, most of the time we simply dug out and discarded all the red, brick-like clay because it drains so poorly. Here in Florida, the problem is usually the opposite; the soil—mostly sand—drains too well, retaining insufficient moisture and nutrients to feed and water the plant. Either way, the result is the same: the existing soil is removed and the rose is planted in a mixture of humus, peat, top soil or good garden soil, along with organic fertilizer such as Milorganite™ or cow manure.

The subject of soil is important, because roses absolutely must have good drainage. The "blue clay" found in Florida and the "red clay" of Virginia, the Carolinas, Georgia and elsewhere are unsuitable, first because neither drains well and second, because their make-up, their porosity, is such that it's all but impossible to break them up enough to mix in the other ingredients that roses need.

Rootstocks for roses do vary with climate, specifically with temperature. 'Fortuniana' and 'Dr. Huey' are the two most widely-used rootstocks. Mostly in the Southeast where temperatures are mild—without severe winter freezing—'Fortuniana' rootstock roses are recommended. Although 'Fortuniana' cannot tolerate hard freezing without winter protection of the bud union, 'Dr. Huey' can. Even so, in the north where temperatures are very severe, the budwood (the top growth of the rose, just above the graft) must be protected from freezing by some means: soil or mulch piled like a small hill to protect the bud union/graft from severe cold, or cones made for this purpose that are filled with mulch or soil and peat moss.

Of course, there are those areas in between that do experience freezing temperatures, but not severe enough to require the extra winter protection. In southern Virginia and the Carolinas we never took extra measures to protect the roses from freezing weather. The roses went into dormancy, which was natural, and every winter some canes froze, which also was natural. Each year they were pruned back to healthy wood in early spring, and the cycle of growth and bloom proceeded.

Freezing weather is one reason many people swear by own-root roses that, after all, have been around for millions of years. A rose growing on its own rootstock can stand a lot of freezing, because even if the entire plant above the ground freezes, chances are that come spring the bush will spring up from its root system and you'll still have the same rose. This is not true of either 'Fortuniana' or 'Dr. Huey.' On a bush grafted or budded to either of them (or to any other rootstock), if the bush freezes back to the bud union, all that will be left will be the rootstock, because the bush beginning at the bud union or point of graft simply is no more. It's been frozen. In regions where deep, severe freezing is the norm, even some proponents of own-root roses advise hilling, mounding or using cones filled with mulch or a similar product for protection against the weather. The advantage, they say, is not necessarily to keep from losing the bush to winter kill, but to simply get a quicker start with regrowth in the spring.

Growers differ widely in their approaches to pruning. Generally, in areas where roses go into dormancy, they are not pruned in the fall because if a warm spell should come along in late fall or very early spring (which happens quite often), the bushes get "fooled" into thinking it's time to push out new growth. If and when temperatures drop again, this very tender new growth will be frozen back severely. So if you live in a temperate zone, leave them be—even when they look their worst—until the last danger of a severe frost or freeze is past. Then prune. Here in Florida, where both 'Fortuniana' and 'Dr. Huey' rootstocks are used, those growers who advocate seasonal pruning do it in late January or early February, oftentimes depending upon the weather forecast.

Most of the time, with most bushes, we favor less pruning as opposed to more, simply because every time we cut a rose, regardless of the time of year, we do it with an eye to pruning. In this way, twiggy, immature growth is removed all along. As a result, our bushes are kept at relatively the same size and we eliminate the necessity of drastic, overall pruning at any one time of year.

There are many schools of thought concerning what to use (or not to use), when to spray, how to spray, how often, et cetera. Conditions vary so widely from one area of the state or country to another that it's best to ask specific questions in your local area if you do not find the answers to your questions in the chapter on Caring for Roses.

There is really no substitute for being truly observant of the bushes. Their language may be a little different from your neighbor's, nevertheless, their message constantly hovers over the bushes, inviting those of us who tend them to listen, and then to respond with love and care, sooner than later.

Growing Roses with... BILL & MARY MAUD SHARPE

"We began growing roses because a friend came to visit, went with us to Thomasville Nurseries* (Thomasville, Georgia) to select plants and helped us plant our first bed. We've made many mistakes along the way, but continue to learn more about roses and have met many good rosarian friends.

"We soon learned from our first bed that we should arrange the bushes so that we did not need to walk in the bed to tend the roses. We also learned that because of our clay soil, we needed to plant in raised beds. With time we have learned many of the varieties that do best in our north Florida location. Nursery growers have given us tips on spraying and fertilizing that have helped us save money and grow better roses. We try to keep abreast of the information on good cultural practices from the American Rose Society Consulting Rosarian program. We have made an effort to grow all kinds of roses and have used garden structures such as poles, trellises and a wooden fence.

"Various plantings of camellias, azaleas, daylilies and other perennials and annuals add to the landscaping of our garden.

"We recommend visits to other gardens, and at the same time suggest that those who need help seek advice from others who are successfully growing roses. Sharing a rose with a friend, and having that friend become a rose lover and grower can be a rewarding experience."

*Unfortunately no longer in business.

*Runnin' east t'ward summer's sun
Mama's picket fence...
Dotted red with roses.*

THE NECESSITY OF SPACE

One of the first sermons I remember distinctly was in the small, southern Virginia town where my childhood was spent. Of course it was in a Baptist church, there being three times as many churches of this denomination in the area as any other. The preacher's name was Dr. McCabe. He was not only a preacher, but a farmer, a big man with a deep, resonant voice. On this occasion, a Sunday morning in early summer, he walked from behind the pulpit and stood as close to the congregation as possible. He said, "I've been told there's been some talking about what I raise on my farm. Well, like most other farmers in these parts, I grow two main crops: tobacco and corn." He looked out over the congregation as if he were memorizing every face in the church. He even raised his eyes to the balcony, where I was hanging onto the rail trying to hear every word. Then he raised his hands and said, slowly and deliberately, "My brothers, don't do as I do, do as I say."

'Orangeade' Floribunda

It was a long time before I understood the significance of those words. He'd been preaching against smoking and either making or drinking corn whiskey, yet he was growing tobacco and corn on his own farm. I could not help but think of Dr. McCabe this week when I suddenly realized that I'm guilty of the very thing I've "preached" against—planting rose bushes too close for comfort—both their comfort and ours.

When we first laid out our garden, we planted the bushes six feet apart in a raised bed. This provided ample space to maneuver between the bushes for watering, spraying, cutting, fertilizing and other garden chores, and is recommended to those planning a new garden. Unfortunately, in our case it did not last. When, from time to time, I'd get "just one more bush," a spot had to be found to squeeze it in somewhere, and when we'd lose a bush— which is inevitable every now and then—it would usually be replaced not with one bush but with two! In time our garden became so overplanted that it was difficult to walk between many of the plants. That's when we decided something had to be done to rectify the situation.

We looked at the garden layout for weeks and even considered removing some bushes, but then decided to approach the problem from another angle. Perhaps we could create islands of rosebushes with winding paths between them. We marked out a couple of experimental paths with a garden hose to see if the idea looked workable. It did, so we began pruning bushes on the side facing the path, thus making space to tend the roses, and to keep from tearing up the bushes and ourselves by being caught amongst the canes. We created the paths by applying an extra-thick covering of mulch, about six to eight inches. Keeping roses along the pathway pruned is an ongoing challenge, but the paths have made working in the garden much easier. And much to our surprise, the bushes don't look lopsided, because almost every plant has others touching it on two to three sides.

While our crowding problem has been alleviated, the new arrangement's a compromise and we still can't easily get to every side of every bush. Though this is sometimes inconvenient, the bushes don't seem to be suffering. Careful observation has given us no reason to suspect that the roots are crowded. The foliage is heavy and is a vibrant, healthy green. Master basals continue to emerge and the garden is a glorious rainbow of roses. But as Dr. McCabe says, don't do as I do, do as I say!

'Cécile Brünner' Hybrid Polyantha

'Hannah Gordon' Floribunda

And that is to leave ample space between your rose-bushes—at least six feet, preferably more.

Besides providing adequate access for maintenance chores, another reason to give rosebushes plenty of "elbow room" is to discourage the spread of disease. The garden of our neighbors Lynn and Rusty Woods provides an example. A few years ago, the Woods' garden was struck a deadly blow by downy mildew (as was ours and many other gardens in the area). The Woods applied specialized sprays as soon as the fungus was identified, but it was already too late for many of the bushes. Some died immediately and others were left in such a weakened condition that it was only a matter of time before they also succumbed. The Woods' decision about what to do was not long in coming. They pulled out all the bushes, burned them, hauled in fresh soil and mulch, purchased new plants and started over—but with a difference. Half again as much space was left between the plants as in their first garden. This not only made spraying easier and more efficient, it allowed more exposure to sunlight and better air circulation between the bushes, discouraging fungus and mildew and slowing the transmission from bush to bush of any blight that might crop up.

That year, downy mildew claimed all of our bushes with the exception of seven: two 'Hannah Gordon' bushes, 'Permanent Wave,' 'Cécile Brünner,' 'Carefree Beauty,' 'Orangeade,' and one 'Don Juan.' Even though these seven were affected, they were strong enough to pull through, and I am thankful to say they're still strong, healthy and producing beautiful roses to this day.

When it comes to growing roses
Are we purists or piddlers,
Or are we in that grand garden somewhere in between?

Roses must have soil that drains readily. However, since most Florida soil is overly sandy, to grow outstanding roses it must be amended—replaced actually—with soil mixed from scratch. A good soil mix for roses contains topsoil, humus or sphagnum peat moss, and manure (dehydrated commercial or pasture)—roughly one-third each. These ingredients should be thoroughly mixed and ready before planting.

Regardless of soil or climate, roses must have abundant water and will not grow and bloom well without it; however, they cannot tolerate wet feet. Even several days of standing water or soggy conditions around the plants can cause severe damage. Therefore, it's wise to plant in raised beds or where there is no danger of water accumulating.

To plant a standard-sized rosebush, dig a hole 20 inches wide and 20 inches deep. Retain about one-fourth of the removed soil, and combine it thoroughly with the already-prepared, humus-rich soil mix. Before refilling the hole, toss in a scant handful of superphosphate and a cup (or so) of bone meal. Mix these ingredients in the bottom of the hole, and then refill it about halfway to the top with the soil mixture. Remove the rosebush from its container and place the root ball on top of the filled-in soil. Adjust the height of the root ball in the hole by adding or subtracting soil from the hole. At this point, water thoroughly and let all the water sink in before adding more soil. The root ball should be about one to two inches above ground level, because over a period of time the root ball will sink. If the top of the root ball sinks below ground level, pretty soon soil will fill in around the trunk, a condition that can cause it to rot or encourage insect infestation. Continue filling the hole around the root ball. Firm the soil around the root ball, but do not pack it down too tightly.

Some rose growers include granular fertilizer in the hole at planting time, but I do not, for fear of burning tender feeder roots. A safer method is to sprinkle a scant handful of fertilizer on top of the ground all the way around the bush after planting is completed. Rain or watering will gradually work this top-dressing of fertilizer down through the soil.

Once the soil has been firmed all around the root ball, water thoroughly. Water every day for one week, then every two days for another week. By this time, new growth will probably emerge. In another week, a second scant handful of fertilizer should be spread around the bush, six to eight inches out from the trunk.

A newly-planted rose bush should not bloom for at least the first month, so cut off the first small buds as they form, but do not cut long stems. Leave as many canes and as much foliage as possible, remembering that limbs and foliage are a rose's food factory. Removing early buds will aid the plant in producing more foliage, so that it will more quickly become a heavy, bushy plant.

We try to give every rosebush we get the best of everything, but sometimes opportunity strikes when no preparations have been made for it. One day in early January, a 'Don Juan' bush in bud and bloom was given to us as a gift. It so happened that at the time we had no peat moss, no superphosphate, no topsoil already dug. We were ill-prepared to plant a rose, other than having a bed in which to plant it. But then I thought of Mel Bough, who had said more than once, "Roses will take more than you might think. It pays not to be too particular."

So off we went to our pasture to gather a five-gallon bucket of natural cow cakes. We returned to the rosebed, dug a hole, removed the sand, and proceeded to plant the bush with nothing but natural cow manure and water: no peat moss, no compost, nothing except the pasture cow cakes. We have never had a rose respond any more vigorously or rapidly, and our 'Don Juan' is still excelling in growth and blooms. It's over eight feet tall, has multiple new basals, and is a truly happy rose. So, while not generally recommending such planting procedures for roses, I have to admit that we just may try this again, sometime.

In giving you this red, red rose
It gives back to me your joy.

The ideal time to move or transplant an established rosebush is when the weather is cool. In a temperate climate like Florida's, the cooler the temperature the better. In other climates, it's best to transplant in early autumn or early spring, when the bush is dormant but the ground is not frozen. Of course, picking the season when you'll transplant a rose is not always possible, if the reason is the sale of a house or an unanticipated, extended absence from home and garden. The bigger and older a bush is, the more difficult it is to satisfactorily transplant it, but roses don't give up easily and it is usually worth the effort to try to move a rose, especially if it's an unusual variety or a treasured plant.

At least 90 days prior to the move, a rosebush should be root pruned using a sharp shooter spade. Drive the spade into the ground in a circular pattern around the bush, allowing about eight to ten inches radius for each one inch of cane diameter. Repeat the root pruning every three to four weeks during the 90-day period. This will force the rose to develop new roots within that circle, which will help sustain it after it is moved.

The new planting hole should be dug and ready to receive the rosebush ahead of time. Before moving the rose, water it thoroughly and cut off or prune about one-third to one-half the canes, removing all buds and blooms. Then dig the rose quickly, keeping as much soil intact around the roots as possible. To help keep the soil from falling away from the roots, wrap the ball in burlap or other heavy fabric that's been soaked in water. Position the bush in its new hole, firming soil around and over the root ball and watering generously. Burlap will quickly rot away in the ground so there's no need to remove it. However, if you use a heavier material to wrap the root ball, it's best to cut the material away after placing the bush in the hole. If the bush seems wobbly in the new hole, stake it on at least two sides. Shade the bush for two to three weeks or until new growth begins to appear. Keep the bush well watered, but not waterlogged, and do not fertilize it for several weeks.

A mature rose that has been dug up and replanted is unlikely to recover sufficiently the first season to bloom prolifically. The important thing is that it develops new growth with strong canes and foliage, so that when the next season rolls around, it will be ready to produce its "show" again.

It is very difficult to successfully transplant bare root roses except when they are dormant—that is, without foliage. For this reason, most growers that sell bare root roses through catalogs ship them only from late fall to early spring. Very few garden centers sell bare root bushes because it is so difficult to keep these plants fresh for any length of time. The canes and roots of bare root bushes start drying out from the moment they're dug, so they are sometimes waxed to retard evaporation. Even then, stocking them is a gamble that most nurseries don't want to take.

Container-grown roses that are well-established and have an ample network of feeder roots can be transplanted any time of year in temperate climates. In cold climates where the ground is more or less frozen through wintertime it would be impossible to dig and properly plant them. Even if they could be planted, it would serve no purpose since the rose cannot grow in the dead of winter, thus this should not be a consideration.

Some roses seem to delight in being transplanted. For instance, my friend Dot Jackson, who writes and grows roses in Six Mile, South Carolina, kept telling me about her "Cracker" rose that was coming up "everywhere" in her yard. "It even poked its longest, winding cane through a big crack beside my bedroom window!" she said. From her description of the rose over the phone, I thought it might be 'Lady Banksia' but couldn't be sure, so she said, "I'll send you one." I really didn't think she'd go to all that trouble, but in less than a week, the mail brought a bedraggled brown envelope containing a six-inch rose cane with two straggly leaflets and a small bunch of roots around which Dot had wrapped a gluey handful of damp red clay. It was a sad-looking little plant. I immediately put it in a pot with good soil, being careful not to disturb the clump of red dirt around its roots, and placed it where it would receive morning sun. In less than a week new sprouts started emerging, and within a month it produced seven new leaflets and a brand new basal cane. It didn't seem to mind a bit traveling in a beat-up brown envelope through the US Mail to be transplanted in the backwoods subtropics of Florida.

Dot's traveling "Cracker" rose is reminiscent of stories about our pilgrim ancestors bringing slips of roses across the ocean from their home country, so they would have rose reminders in their new homeland of America. Years later, cuttings from these first bushes were tucked in among the belongings of their descendants, on the covered wagons that trekked westward. In this way, some of the oldest roses of the old country, some dating back to the sixteenth and seventeenth centuries, were transplanted anew. Early pioneers carried short cuttings with one end stuck into a potato or an apple to keep them moist and alive until they could be planted.

Many of these durable, centuries-old roses are sweetly fragrant and able to weather the elements of heat and cold, drought and flood. Often they are very old but rather common varieties, remarkably free of diseases, easy to root, with an extraordinary, ingrown sense of survival. This makes them extremely easy to care for and very desirable.

"Rose rustlers" are groups of rosarians that ride through the countryside, looking specifically for roses that fall into this category. The types of places most likely to possess such cultivars are deserted cemeteries, along fallen-down fencerows, near abandoned houses, sheds and barns, and in remote churchyards. Rose-rustling groups rarely if ever try to dig a rose; instead, they take canes from ungrafted Old Garden Roses and from them make further cuttings to root and start new bushes. These rooted beginnings may be planted and transplanted any number of times before finally finding a home. Identification comes later when the rooted cuttings finally bloom. These old garden roses—truly antiques—have been found throughout the West, but because the art of "rustling" had its beginnings in the Lone Star State, more have been found there than anywhere else. Although the original Texas Rose Rustlers cared little about the formal classifications of the "rose world," they discovered true adventure in their quest for little-known and historically interesting rose varieties, and some now say that rose rustling has grown into a big business.

After the flight of the frightening storm…
Like hope—a rainbow over the garden.

STAKING

When we grew roses "up yonder" in Virginia and North Carolina, we never gave a thought to staking. Not so, here in this land of brisk breezes and not infrequent storms, with our garden full of long-necked bushes grafted on 'Fortuniana.' The year-round growing season in much of Florida allows most bushes, regardless of rootstock, to grow so big that staking is a necessity. (When I inquired why 'Fortuniana' "necks" were so long, the surprising answer was "just to be different from those bushes grafted onto other rootstocks"! Later, upon noting that 'Fortuniana' grafts on Jackson & Perkins roses were just the same as other rootstock grafts, I made further inquiries and learned that, indeed, the long neck serves no purpose.)

In Florida's heat and damp, what sort of stakes will last and will not harm the bush? Sturdy tomato stakes are fine, but they are relatively short-lived. Rot-resistant cypress stakes are great, if they can be obtained without cutting trees. Many low-hanging cypress limbs are large enough to make excellent rose stakes. Rebar is one of the very best materials, provided that the bar is encased in a length of rubber garden hose to keep the metal from coming in contact with the trunk or limbs of the rose.

For a long time now, rose companies have labeled their bushes with tags attached to the trunk with metal wire. This ensures the tag's longevity, but sooner or later this metal wire will cause a toxic reaction in the rose. Dieback occurs at the point of contact and usually spreads. This toxic effect may not occur for months or even years, but our experience has been that it happens eventually. Canes or trunks may also be killed by girdling when the wire becomes imbedded. Therefore, we promptly remove such wires and reattach the ID tag with string or plastic tape. Old nylon stockings cut into strips work just fine and are not highly visible. They won't harden and break like plastic.

Like an Oriental painting…
Petals bobbing on the pond…
A fleet of little white boats.

3. Caring for Roses

THE BASIC NEEDS

Caring for roses in Florida or elsewhere is a matter of following a few simple rules with a modicum of common sense—and considerable love for the rose itself.

The requirements of your roses once they are in the ground are listed here, not necessarily in order of importance. They are:

— Food/fertilizer
— Water
— General spraying/pest and disease control
— Pruning/shaping/deadheading
— Careful observation (very important!)

It is one thing to walk in the garden, enjoying the beauty and fragrance of the roses, but quite another to walk in the garden and really comprehend what is going on and what is not going on—in other words, to genuinely perceive their conditions, their state of health, happiness and well being.

A rose grower of no little note who grew hundreds of superb roses in Southwest Florida some few years ago (who had to build an addition onto his home to house all his trophies), said to me more than once: "If you learn to recognize their language, to 'hear' and become aware of what they are saying… through sight, touch, and even smell, they will tell you what you need to know in terms of what they need from you." About their scent, he continued, "This is not a notion. Numbers of times when a traditionally very fragrant rose seemed to suddenly become less fragrant… less pleasing, I knew this was not normal… that the bush was not in a healthy state. Most of the time I discovered that for whatever reason that particular bush was not getting the water it needed. A rose that's thirsty, even slightly dehydrated, will definitely not exhibit the same level of fragrance."

And then he'd say in one way or another, "As rose growers… keepers of the garden… we need to learn to grasp mentally what's going on with our family of rose bushes. Then correct the hill of the problem before it becomes a mountain."

Then he reached down and touched a rose, saying, "Being truly observant is a part of the success process of growing these very special flowers."

You will soon find that there are countless "extras"—both products and techniques—that may be incorporated into your care regimen to the extent you desire. Experience is the best teacher and you will find that you learn the most by doing, but to get you started here is a primer on each of the basic requirements.

Feeding

There are many schools of thought on feeding roses—maybe too many! The most basic tenet is that any plant which produces as much as roses do, especially in warm climates, must be fed and watered often enough to "feed its habit" of constant giving, otherwise the plant will suffer, resulting in fewer blooms of less quality. If you do nothing else except buy a bag of fertilizer designated as "rose food" or "rose fertilizer" and apply it regularly as recommended on the bag, you will have at least provided food for the bush that will aid in its sole reason for being: to grow and produce roses for you to enjoy!

How often should you fertilize? The once-a-month schedule is probably the most popular. This was our schedule for some years. However, when we began noticing slightly pale foliage and less vigorous growth about two to three weeks after feeding, we began using less fertilizer but applying it more frequently—specifically, every three weeks. The bushes definitely responded, holding their color and vigor better. One of Florida's most knowledgeable rose growers has said more than a few times: "Learn to look at your roses… really observe them. While they cannot talk in our language, they can, and will, tell you what they need."

There are fine growers who firmly recommend feeding every two weeks, without deviation, and we cannot disagree with this. We follow a three-week schedule rather than a two-week one to save time. The soil a rose is planted in makes a big difference in how often it needs to be fed. The higher the porosity of the soil, the more fertilizer roses require, since nutrients will tend to leach away more quickly.

That old saying, "Never feed a sick person or plant" is more than just a saying. It's gospel truth in the garden. Feeding a sick plant only makes the plant's condition worse. Roots of an ailing plant cannot tolerate food—fertilizer. Keep the bush well watered, but do not feed it. However, a hungry plant isn't necessarily a sick plant. Plants that need feeding usually exhibit pale green foliage rather than strong green, especially in areas of new growth.

Some growers heartily recommend an extra feeding of soluble fertilizer at any time a bush looks "hungry"—that is, it has pale leaves, weak new growth or a tendency to catch every fungus spore that blows into the garden! At these times, even if a little extra soluble fertilizer doesn't seem to help, it won't hurt. However, this doesn't mean to ignore directions, which usually vary somewhat from one brand of fertilizer to another. If used as the primary source of nutrients, most soluble fertilizers must be applied every few days or every week for optimum results.

There are all sorts of fertilizers specifically manufactured for roses. On the other hand, there are dozens of fertilizers that, though not specifically labeled for roses, will work just fine. For instance, for years we have been using a 17-5-11 fertilizer that doesn't have the word "rose" on the bag anywhere. Nevertheless, it does the job better than several others we have used from time to time.

Other formulations of granular fertilizers that suit roses are 15-4-10, 12-6-8, 10-6-12 (Ace), 8-4-8 (Gro-tone™), 15-12-15 (Bethel Farms' Rose Grow™), plus others. The first and third numbers of each "guaranteed analysis" denote the proportions of nitrogen and potassium, respectively, and should be higher than the second number, which indicates the relative amount of phosphorus.

Many home gardeners ask "Should fertilizer with systemic insecticide, or fertilizer without, be used?" There are many successful rose growers in both schools, but most prefer fertilizer without systemic insecticide for several reasons, not the least of which is cost. Fertilizer with systemic insecticide is considerably more expensive and is of very little or no value for rose bushes exceeding six feet in height, since the insecticide is ineffective more than six feet from the root. The latter restriction eliminates its effectiveness on bushes such as 'Don Juan' and other Climbers, as well as tall bushes like 'Lady of the Dawn,' 'Hannah Gordon,' 'Permanent Wave' and many more. In addition to these considerations, we don't use fertilizer with systemic insecticide because we heartily believe in using insecticide only when there are obvious signs that it's needed, and then selecting the appropriate treatment for the specific pest.

Another consideration where fertilizer is concerned is whether to use a time-release type. Here again, cost can be a factor, but saving one's time and energy should also be considered. Time-release fertilizers can be a godsend for those who are away from home and garden for long periods of time due to travel or seasonal residency.

The feeding period of time-release fertilizers varies quite a bit, from one to nine months. Temperature and moisture cause the pellets to slowly break down, providing a continuous release of nutrients into the soil for the duration of the feeding period. In addition to convenience, another benefit of time-release fertilizer is that, according to most manufacturers, there's no need to worry about overfeeding or underfeeding when directions are followed. A case in point: We came by a new rose food that claimed to continue feeding effectively for six months. I was a classic doubting Thomas! However, after using this fertilizer in a designated area in our garden over a six-month period, and observing and comparing results, we came to the conclusion that every word the manufacturer claimed was true. The

Growing Roses with... LYNN & RUSTY WOODS

"There are many different levels of commitment in the art of growing roses. For reasons of time or inclination, many people want a few rose bushes in their yard and an occasional bloom to take in the house. I say this is perfectly fine, but should be recognized by the grower from the outset. This person should invest the least amount for the bushes by going to a discount center, spray when he or she remembers, fertilize and water occasionally, enjoy the blooms, and treat the bushes as disposable plants. Replant as necessary!

"There are some rose growers who are very serious and will go to great lengths in the quest for a prize at a rose show. Then there are people like my husband and me. We have no desire to show our roses, except to our friends, but we want prize-winning blooms for our own enjoyment. My thoughts here are addressed to this group.

"Yes, one can grow lovely roses in South Florida! Our garden is in the southwest quadrant of Glades County. However, like most worthwhile projects, it is not easy. If you are truly committed to being a good grower, start with very good (not cheap) plants from a reputable garden center staffed by knowledgeable people. Get all the information they have about planting, fertilizing, pest control, and pruning. Join the local chapter of the American Rose Society. There is absolutely no substitute for advice from experienced growers who are growing in your environment!

"Remember the old adage about 'you get what you pay for'? Well, that certainly holds true for rose growing. If you want your bushes to work hard, you must feed them regularly with a top grade fertilizer. Follow the instructions in this book and set up a work routine when you plant your first bush. Whatever effort you put into your rose-growing you will get back the rewards tenfold if you 'do it right.'"

Author's note: At the deadline for this book, the Woods' home and gardens have been sold. Fortunately, the new owners, Ann and Terry Starck, cherish the gardens and are learning quickly what to do and not to do. Although growing roses is new to them, it seems safe to say that not only have the roses passed into good hands, but so has the love for them.

product is Rose Grow™, a time-release rose fertilizer from Bethel Farms; its guaranteed analysis is 15-12-15. Another highly respected time-release plant food, Osmocote™, has a feeding period of nine months. It is available in various formulations, several of which suit roses fine.

Also, there are those (we among them) who believe in applying cow manure, in any of its forms, often. Real often! Every two months is not one day too frequent. One way to apply it is in a concoction called "cow tea." The recipe is simple: In a five-gallon bucket (or better still, in a big garbage can) soak cow cakes in water for several days. Pour the resulting "tea" around the bushes. That old saying "If a little is good, a lot is better" does apply where cow tea is concerned, but it does not apply to commercial or chemical fertilizers.

The highly-respected, nationally acclaimed "Rosarian Rambler," Mr. Howard Walters of Greenville, South Carolina, is a great believer in cow tea for many good reasons. He says: "Unlike commercial fertilizer, 'cow tea,' as well as alfalfa tea and fish emulsion solutions, still work the best with roses of all types, including and especially Miniatures. These mixtures feed the soil, supporting the organisms that convert nutrients into forms available to plants. A long chain but a simple one. Food value is built in as well, but the primary boost comes from activating the soil organisms. It cannot burn, and tiny root hairs love it." About this special tea, he says, "If you haven't brewed up one of the Rambler's 'teas,' your roses haven't enjoyed a natural and highly beneficial treat."

Other additives that aid in the healthy growth of roses include Epsom salts (magnesium sulfate), superphosphate, potash (potassium sulfate) and water. First, last, and always, water!

Consider all the options regarding fertilizers, then experiment in your own garden to find what works best for you.

Watering

An efficient irrigation system is a marvelous thing, but we do not have one. From time to time, it's been suggested that such a system would make a grand birthday or Christmas gift, and I agree that it would. Yet, when water from "upstairs" is in short supply, the few hours spent in hand watering are truly enjoyable—and valuable. Watering time is thinking time, with some dreaming included for good measure. It is also close-inspection time. As we water each bush all the way 'round, we closely go over it, limb by limb, to check for bugs and blights, diseases and deadwood. By so doing, we usually can keep ahead of major problems.

Still, an irrigation system is a lovely convenience, and if you have included one in your rose garden plans, go that extra mile and see to it that the water for each bush is released by jet-spray in a way that distributes water evenly around the entire plant, not just on one side. The same principle applies to hand watering: do not water just one side—apply water all around the bush. Roots spread laterally as well as down, and will grow fastest where there is ample water. Providing water evenly around the entire drip line will produce a strong, balanced root system.

How often should you water? You must consider several factors. Naturally, rain is important, but so are temperature and wind. A soaking, mid-summer rain will keep our garden watered for the following two days—longer, if those two days are cloudy and windless. However, if those two days are hot and windy, we will water the second day. Warm winds inevitably dry both soil and bushes, therefore when windy conditions prevail, take extra care in seeing that roses have ample water. When there's no rain at all, we water every two to three days depending upon wind and temperature. To determine how often to water, feel of the soil around the base of the plant. If it's damp to the touch, that's fine; if it's dry, water. Feel of the same soil the next day and so on until you determine how often roses need watering. You will probably have to adjust your schedule periodically. Winter is usually the dry season in Florida, which means that we'll water about every three days. However, if temperatures are unusually high, and as a result the bushes look a little limp and thirsty, we'll water every other day.

When a garden is first planted and the bushes have not yet become established, it will not take much time nor effort to determine how often your roses need watering. Feel of the soil around the bushes and observe the foliage carefully. If the leaves look the least bit limp and droopy, it's time to water. Apply a minimum of three to four gallons per watering, or three to four inches per week if you're using an irrigation system.

A rose that wilts from lack of water is in dire distress. When this happens, the bush is likely to never fully recover. Keen observation will allow you to notice thirst before wilting occurs. The slightest bending of new growth, particularly new buds, should alert you that the plant needs water. Mature foliage that has a lackluster, papery appearance is another sign of thirst.

It's been said that it's difficult to overwater a bush with proper drainage, but this is not completely accurate. After all, one can water a bush to the point that all nutrients are leached from the soil, and that's too much. And to water a bush so often that the soil continually stays soggy will kill the bush sooner rather than later. Although roses will not tolerate "wet feet," neither can they tolerate bone-dry conditions for any length of time, so avoid sprinkling as opposed to thoroughly watering. Sprinkling wets only the top inch or so of soil and in time, if this practice is continued, the tiny, white feeder roots tend to gravitate to the surface because they are attracted to the moisture. Then, if and when the top soil is allowed to dry out or becomes hot, these tender roots will quickly die off. This is damaging since these feeder roots, as their name implies, carry nourishment to the bush. In contrast, the heavy, brown roots support the plant.

Perhaps it doesn't need to be said again, but some of the most knowledgeable and devoted growers we know say, "Don't let your roses wilt." Wilting stresses plants, making them more likely to produce small blooms without good substance, and it makes them more susceptible to blights and bugs. Continual thirst will kill a bush far more quickly than hunger.

There is considerable difference of opinion as to whether one should rinse the leaves of rose bushes, particularly in very hot weather. We think it's helpful. Invariably, when buds begin to bend over in the stifling heat of an 80- to 90-degree day, a cooling spray of water from the hose will bring them out of a wilt in less than 30 minutes. Naturally, it makes no sense to do this when the roses have just been sprayed. However, if information on certain chemical labels is correct, after only eight hours systemically-effective ingredients have already entered a plant's system, so water will not render the spraying ineffective.

Do not spray roses or wash foliage late in the day, because if foliage stays wet overnight, the moisture will encourage development of fungus diseases. Early morning is best for watering and spraying, before temperatures rise above 70 degrees.

General Spraying

It's far easier and much more satisfactory from every standpoint to practice preventive maintenance than it is to wait until diseases or insects attack your roses and then wonder what to do. For controlling fungus and disease, a sensible, regular spray program is the golden rule to follow. Such a program will lessen or prevent the occurrence of fungi like blackspot, powdery and downy mildews, rust, and botrytis blight, as well as bacterial diseases that affect roses.

Before spraying, it's very important to pick off any unhealthy-looking foliage and dispose of it. It does little, if any, good to spray roses unless diseased foliage has first been removed. Also, as a preventive measure, never let diseased foliage accumulate on the ground around bushes. This will only add problems. Don't put collected rose foliage or cuttings in compost, because fungus spores (and some insects) thrive in a moist, warm environment; they could later cause problems when the compost is used, either as a planting medium or in combination with mulch. Dispose of rose foliage and cuttings as you would garbage, or in a burn bin.

Also, be sure that bushes are well watered before spraying. Thirsty bushes can easily be burned or injured with spray materials. A good rule of thumb is to water the bushes the day or night before spraying.

About sprayers, the late rose grower Richard Hedenberg said: "A good sprayer is a necessary investment for every rose grower. For a small or beginning garden, a one- or two-gallon compression pump-up sprayer with a long wand works well. Select one with a funnel top for easier filling. Don't select a sprayer larger than you can comfortably carry. Water is surprisingly heavy and the larger the sprayer, the heavier it will be. Sprayers on the market for domestic garden use range from pump-up types to rechargeable battery-powered types with a capacity of many gallons that come on a wheeled cart, to electrically-powered blower types that blast a fine mist and provide excellent coverage to both the top and underside of foliage. The mister-type sprayers are also the most economical for the small amount of spray material they use as compared to the other types. This makes them cost effective in the long run. Probably the best advice is to select one you can easily handle to start with."

Two gallons of spray material do a good job for a garden the size of ours. For our hundred or so bushes, we use a polyethylene one-gallon pump sprayer. One of the secrets for this type of sprayer is to keep it well pumped, so that the spray material is dispensed in a fine spray-mist. Our Spray Doc™ has a filter that must be kept clean, and it works very well provided it's cleaned after every use. We would not buy any sprayer without a filter! Because water and chemicals may contain foreign matter, even with a filter it's a good idea to place a clean cloth over the mouth of the sprayer when filling it, to keep out any sediment or impurities. Even minute particles can clog a sprayer, so the more that are kept out, the better.

Our "recipe" for a gallon of spray is this: To one quart of warm water, add 1 tablespoon Funginex™, 1 scant tablespoon Dithane M45™, and 2 tablespoons Rose Defense™ (derived from neem oil). These ingredients mix much better in warm water, and it's easier to mix them in a wide-mouthed quart jar so that they may be stirred vigorously. We've also discovered that the mixing is best when the Dithane M45™ (a powder) is added to the water first and stirred, then the Funginex™ (a liquid) is stirred in,

Growing Roses with...
EULA AND CARROLL RICHARDS

ARS Consulting Rosarians, National ARS Judges, winners of national, state, regional and local awards, Eula and Carroll Richards live in their garden of 200-plus roses in North Fort Myers. Eula was awarded the 2000 Outstanding Consulting Rosarian Award, Deep South District. The Richards devotion, advice and recommendations are unquestioned them.

The Richards on the subject of spraying:

"BLACKSPOT: Spray faithfully every seven days. Use 1 tsp./gal. Triforene and 1 tbs./gal. Manzate 200™. If Funginex™ is used (instead of Triforene™) the rate is 1 tbs./gal. and if Dithane™ is used (instead of Manzate 200™) use 1 tbs./gal. If a bad case of blackspot moves in, as mentioned above, spray more frequently. However, never increase or double spray formulation which can cause spray burn and may damage roses severely.

"THRIPS: Use a hand spray bottle and mist buds every other day when color first appears. Continue until thrips disappear. Effective insecticides for thrips are Mavrik™, Orthene™ or Cygon 2E™ at ¼ tsp./quart. Mavrik™ takes care of aphids, corn ear worms and leaf worms as well as thrips. Thuricide™ can also be used for corn ear worms at ½ tsp./quart. Important: only spray the growth of the plant that is infested.

"SPIDER MITES: This is the most destructive mite for roses in summer. Mites are not insects, but are related to spiders. Mites and spiders are arachnids, a large group of arthropods with four pairs of legs, lunglike sacs or breathing tubes and a body usually divided into two segments. Thus the remedy for their control is not necessarily the same as for insects.

"In hot weather the life cycle of spider mites can be as short as five days, in which period of time they lay many eggs. The preferred method of control is to disrupt the life cycle with a water wand* that blasts a strong jet of water to the underside of the leaves where the mites breed. This can be done in the heat of the day, which will not only aid bushes with the problem of mites but will freshen and cool them at the same time. Such a blast of water three days in a row will do wonders where mites are concerned. If a chemical control is needed, the preferred miticide is Avid™ at ¼ tsp./gal. One spraying kills mites but not their eggs. After five days, a second spraying will kill the newly hatched mites. It is not recommended to mix Avid™ with other sprays. Water well the day before spraying."

The Richards advise wearing long sleeves, a respirator mask, gloves and eye protection, and recommend laundering clothing after spraying.

*Author's Note: We have found that an ordinary pistol-type trigger nozzle, with water on full force, is more effective than a water wand. We noticed advertisements for various water wands that were said to be ideal for washing bushes in the war against red spider mites, so we bought one. It produced a soft spray of water, ideal for potted plants and soft, frail foliage plants, even roses. It was not, however, ideal for spray-washing bushes to remove spider mites. A traditional, functional hose nozzle is the best thing we've found for this purpose. It's straightforward, easy to use, and readily available at the nearest hardware store.

*The roses are calling and I am falling
into the cobwebs of spring.*

and lastly, the Rose Defense™ (an oil-based liquid) is added. Pour the first quart of water (with chemicals) into the sprayer reservoir, then add the other three quarts of water to make a gallon.

Do not mix fungicides that combat diseases with insecticides that combat insects. Apply insecticide spray only when an insect problem has been detected, and then choose a pesticide that is specific for the insect to be controlled.

Is time of day important when spraying? Absolutely! The earlier the spraying is done, the better. Never spray in late morning or midday. If the temperature is above 72 degrees there is a likelihood of burning foliage. Late-day or evening spraying is also not advisable because, while the temperature may be suitable, the foliage will remain wet overnight, promoting fungus diseases. There is no time as good for spraying roses as early morning. Do not spray when foliage is wet or the spray material will do little good.

Some rose growers, for whom we have great respect, say that products derived from neem oil-based products such as Rose Defense™ will burn foliage "in Florida." We have been trial-using Rose Defense™ for over two years and have not experienced any burning. We are inclined to believe that when spray is applied in early morning, or at other times when temperatures are not above 72 degrees, there is no burning. However, measuring spray ingredients is also crucial—we have never used over two level tablespoons of Rose Defense™ per gallon. It's also very important to keep the spray materials agitated, vigorously shaking the spray canister between every several bushes, and to spray only until the foliage glistens, never until there are droplets and runoff, which could cause burning.

How often should you spray? There are growers who spray faithfully every week—exactly every seven days. There is nothing wrong with this program and it's probably the most foolproof way to keep roses in a disease and insect-free state. Two of the finest growers we know live only a few miles from us. They spray religiously every seven days and there is no question that from this program of care they consistently get fine results, and they have countless awards and accolades to prove their expertise. We spray every seven to ten days, and I must admit that our

garden does not achieve the level of perfection that theirs does. Why do we spray less frequently? The answer is simply that many times our schedule does not allow an exact, every-seven-days spraying. Yet, this does not mean that we do not have healthy, beautiful roses the year 'round.

Over the past several years we have found that our spray schedule is sufficient to keep our roses healthy and happy, with this important caveat: At the first sign of a problem—disease or insect—we immediately get busy and spray with the appropriate chemical, always remembering to thoroughly water the bushes first. If the problem persists, we spray again in three to four days. If this does not remedy the problem, we keep up a three- to five-day spraying schedule until the problem is eradicated. Then we resume the usual schedule.

Where roses grow and bloom during most of the year, the spraying program should be kept up year-round. Even if the blooming cycles seem to slow down a bit in wintertime, bushes that are still fully clothed with foliage should be sprayed. In north Florida, if temperatures fall to freezing and below often enough, roses will drop their foliage, at which time spraying should be ceased until all danger of frost has passed, then resumed. It's very important that new growth be protected while it is disease-free; preventative maintenance is far more satisfactory than allowing a problem to emerge and then trying to alleviate it.

Rainy Day Spraying

In Florida, especially the central and southern regions of the state, the rainy season brings pleasures along with a few problems. This rainy season has a mind of its own as to when it starts and stops. It usually begins in late May or June and ends some time in September or October, yet there seem to be many timetable exceptions.

Many times, we've planned to spray first thing in the morning, only to awaken in the night to the sound of pouring rain on our old tin roof, often continuing 'til daylight—and there goes the plan to spray. On some summer days, clouds will move in quickly around midday and a brief, heavy downpour will follow, although late-afternoon thunderstorms are also very prevalent. The weather keeps us guessing and forces us to be flexible in making our spraying plans.

We try to be faithful to our seven- to ten-day spraying program; however, there are times when Mother Nature has the upper hand and we just can't spray. During these times, we've found that the best thing we can do is to keep the bushes as "clean" as possible. We pick off any beginning diseased leaves every day, keep the deadheads cut, and during times of excessive rain, we provide a little extra fertilizer, knowing that drenching rains quickly leach nutrients from the high-porosity soils that much of Florida has.

Of course, we get back on schedule as quickly as conditions permit. There have been times this year when we have had six to ten rainy days in a row, thus upsetting those best-laid plans of spraying. If we hear a forecast indicating that the next three or four days will be mostly rainy, we spray right then (if there's time), even if we've sprayed just five or six days earlier.

So far we've seen no ill effects from our rainy season routine, and it makes us think how truly extraordinary and rewarding it is to realize how forgiving roses are.

Pruning

In the wild, Mother Nature does her own pruning. When we prune our roses, we are shortcutting her way. Left to their own devices, roses growing in the wild produce strong new shoots/canes from near the base of the bush each year. As they age, lateral, secondary growth from these shoots become weaker. When strong, new canes appear, the plant's food is directed from the roots to the new growth, and consequently, in time, the older canes are starved out. Old growth dies and remains as dead wood before it eventually falls to the ground. Mother Nature's way of pruning travels a long, laborious road but she eventually gets the task done. In our yearly pruning we simply speed up the process, thereby helping our roses to produce more blooms more often.

Pruning roses is necessary for many reasons: to encourage new growth, to re-form an unshapely bush and rebalance the plant, and to rid a bush of diseased canes or deadwood.

More than a few times, we have pruned a sickly plant severely to try and save it. This lessens the workload on the root system that sustains the bush. It's surprising how many times this procedure works. I'm thinking of two during this past year: 'Fragrant Cloud' and 'Ave Maria.' Had these two varieties been readily available for sale, I probably would not have taken the time and energy to try to keep them from the grave. However, I'm delighted to report that both bushes are now large, well and happy, producing dozens and dozens of blooms. Their respective shapes are still not the best, but their production is fine, with perfectly normal blooming cycles and excellent bloom sizes.

During pruning demonstrations we often hear such laments as: "Oh, I can't cut the stems—it might hurt the bush," or "I know my rose would never grow back if I cut it like that!" Responding to such remarks requires lots of patience. But just as there are no two rose bushes exactly alike, there are no two rose growers who prune exactly the same way. There are, however, some general rules and techniques with which most rose growers agree:

Always use sharp, clean tools. Use a pair of hand-held pruners and a small pruning saw. To avoid spreading diseases, fungus spores, bacteria, et cetera, between cuts, it's helpful to dip tools in a bleach solution or to spray them with a small hand sprayer.

As a minimum, remove twiggy, immature growth, dying canes, injured canes, deadwood, and canes that cross and rub against each other. Look carefully at these crossing canes; most of the time one will be inferior to the other, so take out the lesser cane. However, it's not unusual for crossed canes to injure each other to such an extent that both should be cut out.

Cut as close as possible to the cane from which an unwanted twig or cane is growing. Make the cut on a slant, not horizontally, to prevent water from collecting on the cut end and causing it to rot. Before making the next cut, stand back and take a thorough look from all sides at the remaining canes.

In warm climates where roses grow and bloom year-round, it's generally recommended that not more than one-third of the height of a bush be eliminated at one time. This applies to mature

Words of Experience from...
HOWARD WALTERS

Howard Walters lived in Texas prior to moving to Greenville, South Carolina, where he continues to grow roses and to write his "Rosarian Rambler" column in the American Rose, *the monthly magazine of the American Rose Society. He has won many prestigious rose awards, is an accredited ARS judge, an ARS Consulting Rosarian, a popular speaker on the American rose circuit and perhaps most important, a dedicated and devoted rose grower.*

❀ Rose Defense™ is not suitable for Florida where temperatures get too hot and humidity is too high. *(Author's note: We have not found this to be the case in our garden in Florida.)*

❀ Downy mildew requires cold weather to exist, and when temperatures reach 83 degrees, it's gone.

❀ Daconil is the ingredient in several products, but in different concentrations.

❀ Dithane M45™ or T/O and Manzate 200™ are interchangeable; use either one or the other, whichever is available.

❀ Banner Maxx™ is going to be the material of choice to replace Triforine.

❀ The use of Sentinel™ has a downside. It is not labeled for domestic use or for use on roses. *(Author's note: Thus the use of it is illegal.)*

❀ Banner Maxx™ goes after blackspot and powdery mildew in much the same way as Sentinel. Neither product allows spores to duplicate and multiply.

❀ When spraying with Mavrik Aquaflow™, wear a respirator; inhaling it is dangerous.

❀ Use a mite blaster water wand in combination with Avid™ for the best spider mite control.

❀ Stirrup M™ is a sex perfume and a few drops used with a miticide attracts spider mites to it.

❀ Roundup™ is okay for weeds around roses when used in a hand-held spray bottle right down on the weeds you want to kill, and on a calm day. But remember: Roundup™ will kill anything green that it touches. *(Author's note: We do not use Roundup™ or any other herbicide around our roses or in the garden at all. We feel there is a certain danger in doing more harm than good.)*

❀ Use a carry-all for everything you need to mix your spray formulations: pesticides, measuring implements and protective gloves.

❀ Buffering water with Indicate 5™ makes the water "wetter" (i.e., lowers the surface tension), disperses the chemicals better, and adjusts the pH of the water.

❀ Buffer water first, add liquid chemicals next and powders last.

❀ Swirl to blend chemicals in the tank—don't shake. *(Author's note: Since we use Rose Defense™, which is neem oil-based, we shake the tank often to be sure all the materials stay well-mixed.)*

❀ Make long sweeping passes with your spray wand from one side to the other, and then back from top to bottom.

❀ Spray to the point of glistened foliage, but not to the point of excessive run-off.

❀ Don't agitate the spray wand with an up and down motion causing droplets to form; this can burn foliage.

plants, those at least two years old. The reason? Foliage and canes make up the rose's food factory; therefore cutting off more than a third of the bush at one time would rob the rose of too much of its food-production capability.

In the art—and challenge—of pruning, there are shades of difference between Teas, Floribundas, Grandifloras, Climbers and others, as there are differences at times in two bushes of the same variety and the same age. For instance, since most Grandifloras grow tall, it's a good idea to take off about a third of the taller canes, thus forcing out new lower lateral growth. When pruning Climbers, remember that the oldest canes will be the darkest color. Consider the overall size and shape of the plant and if there are several good, strong, vibrant green canes, cut out the oldest, darkest canes. It's the newer canes that will produce the laterals for blooms.

No two growers will prune the same plant in exactly the same way. A backyard grower and a commercial grower have different goals, just as those who primarily grow roses to "show" will use different techniques.

Our personal preference is to leave all major basal canes and some not-so-major ones, if they appear strong and healthy. Ideally, when the pruning task is finished, the bush will have an "open arms" spread from the graft or bud union.

My own philosophy is to prune a little every time a rose is cut. This works nicely for our garden because we are continually "harvesting" roses to share with others, and consequently at no time of year does our garden require a major pruning exercise.

From half a world away, in Orangevale, California, rose grower Baldo Villegas and I are in total agreement regarding whether or not to seal the ends of cut canes. Baldo is the writer of the Beginners' Column in the January 1999 issue of *American Rose*, in which he writes: "Many rosarians recommend sealing cut canes with sealants like weatherproof Elmer's Glue. I personally do not seal the cuts either in winter or the growing season. I have found that if I keep pests like aphids under control, I remove the food that twig-nesting wasps or 'cane borers' use in raising their young—thus no

food, no cane borers! For years we faithfully sealed every cut. Then on a few occasions, for lack of time and thinking we'd get to it later, we didn't. We observed that the cuts healed themselves just fine. Since that time we've never used a sealant." Though it may sound too coincidental, our neighbor Lynn Woods had about the same experience, thus she no longer seals cuts either.

Never, never drop picked-off leaves or "prunings" on the ground with the idea of coming back later and picking them up. Take a plastic pot or bag (with opening wired open) and deposit as you pick. Diseased foliage and canes can quickly infest the "floor" of your garden which will only make for added work later. Enough cannot be said for keeping the garden floor clean and tidy. It may seem like too much work, but it's like a lot of other things: doing a little at a time works wonders. Letting diseased leaves that you pick off or that fall from the bushes stay around your roses invites problems. Many times, for lack of a better place to put them, I'll stuff picked off leaves in my pocket! But most of the time I carry a small bucket into the garden for the purpose.

Again: never, never add rose leaves or cuttings to compost. Here again, diseases and insects can run rampant in such a warm, moist environment. Either burn leaves and cuttings or dispose of them in the garbage where they'll be harmless.

Pruning After a Freeze

It was the third week in January, and we'd just had a hard freeze; the decision had to be made as to when to prune. The temperature had dropped to 22 degrees, and there it stayed for some six to eight hours. Well, that took care of buds and new growth! Much as I wanted to, we did not immediately cut out and clear away the frozen growth. Knowing time would tell and show exactly where to cut the killed-off shoots, we waited—but not patiently.

Such an event brings on see-saw thinking on our part. Would it be wise at this time to do a major pruning job on all the bushes? If we do, we'll be waiting four to six more weeks for roses, but the bushes will be less likely to get nipped if Jack Frost should return. On the other hand, if we let them follow their own natural course, we'll have roses in a couple of weeks. Of course, they may be a bit smaller, but then we have never let size alone be the determining factor concerning what to us is the true beauty and enjoyment of a rose. What a dilemma!

Well, we let Mother Nature take over in her own inimitable way—and as a result, we were soon rewarded with a garden full of roses all at one time. Precisely 14 days later, dead buds had sloughed and new growth had emerged, some up to five inches long. The mature growth was not injured. We carefully inspected each cane for freeze damage, from the tip downward to the point where the new growth had emerged. We removed the damaged parts, cutting to one-fourth inch above the new growth. A couple of days later, there were countless buds all over the garden, some big and fat enough to begin opening within a few days.

Sometimes the cut must go a bit farther down the stem or cane. The cane must be pruned back to good, solid healthy wood. Occasionally a new lateral or two must be cut off, because if the cane is not perfectly healthy, the new lateral will eventually slough anyway.

Every time we're faced with this dilemma I think: Next time we'll do a major job of pruning and then we can compare the two methods with first-hand knowledge. However, we may again be swayed toward having roses sooner, and pruning freeze damage later. Our see-saw deliberations may continue forever.

It's times like these that I am filled with wondrous disbelief at how quickly Mother Nature turns herself around and encourages her charges to reach for the sun, especially in this part of our wonderful world—Glades County, Florida.

Deadheading

Plants, like people, are not at their best all the time. Yet even when they're not, a few buds and blooms are usually evident. To reduce the waiting time between bloom cycles, it's best if deadheads are kept cut off.

As most gardeners know, deadheading is the practice of removing spent flowers in order to improve a plant's appearance and encourage it to generate more blossoms. In deadheading roses, some

growers vow that a rose will actually show where a stem should be cut; the technique requires patience and bears a little explaining. Rather than trying to determine the best place to cut to remove a deadhead, simply snap off or cut the spent bloom right at the neck, just below the bloom. Then wait. Usually in five to seven days, sometimes even less, the bush will start "putting out"—that is, a new lateral will start to emerge at the strongest leaf joint below the spent bloom. There may be more than one of these shoots. If so, it's usually best to snip off the stem just above the biggest one. Some varieties habitually produce clusters of blooms, and when deadheading these you may wish to leave two or more of the largest shoots.

For instance, almost always, 'Sun Flare' sends out multiple shoots, so that in a couple of weeks the bush is a great flare of buttercup yellow buds and blooms. The Climber 'Don Juan' does the same. These two, 'Sun Flare' and 'Don Juan,' "recycle" more quickly than most other roses. We favor the method of snapping off or cutting off spent flowers just below the bloom, particularly when used in conjunction with cutting fresh blooms for the house. The combination demonstrates the advantages of both methods of cutting. When long-stemmed roses are cut for vase use, the remaining canes will be shorter. When blooms are left on the bush to wither, then snapped off, longer canes will result. Therefore the bushes will be shaped high and low, as opposed to maintaining all the canes at about the same height, which some growers prefer.

A continued, heavy wind can bend tall canes, particularly those with heavy buds, some almost into a horseshoe shape. These canes don't usually break, but are too bent to ever straighten themselves. In such cases, apply a lightweight splint to the cane, keeping at least four or five inches both above and below the bend. We often employ a thin twig from an oak sapling for the purpose, using twist ties or masking tape to keep it in place. Once the cane finishes blooming, cut the whole thing off and the bush will produce new laterals at the cut; these, in turn, will produce more blooms.

Rather than cut a heavy cane, particularly a big new one boasting a handsome bloom, often I'll just cut a couple inches below the rose and then float the nearly-stemless flower in a bowl of water. This saves the big cane to do its part in the food-factory chain, producing more laterals and blooms.

Some growers are offended at the sight of a bloom that is even one day beyond its peak of beauty. They can't wait to rid the bushes of spent blooms—but many of us don't get around to deadheading as often as we'd like to, and this raises a question: Does leaving spent blooms on a bush for several days cause any harm? After a good bit of comparing immediate and not-so-immediate deadheading, and asking other growers, we have not found any harm in it, and neither have they. So, to each his own. Most of the time, as long as a bloom is even somewhat colorful, we leave it for its last little fling of beauty in the garden.

As our roses themselves know, as do family and friends, I've been known to cut both buds and blooms from our rosebushes far too much for their own good. But in the last couple years I've tried to mend my ways, and the bushes are duly thankful.

It was 'Permanent Wave,' 'Carefree Beauty' and 'Sun Flare' that captured my attention first. These tend to bloom in an overall burst of color—buds and blooms in all stages at one time. I recall thinking it would be shameful to destroy such a natural bouquet in the garden, and decided to leave them in their natural state of bloom. Thus enlightened, I noticed others that exhibited many of the same characteristics: 'Neon Lights,' 'Betty Prior,' 'Bonica,' 'Europeana,' and many others.

Although all bushes follow a cycle of bloom and recovery, pruning at different times does seem to alter the bloom periods somewhat. I must confess that at times I waffle between wanting all of them to bloom simultaneously or in a sequence. Yet in the final analysis, they're worth waiting for so I don't fret about exactly when they bloom. For the most part, my conclusion is that roses have minds of their own and will bloom in their own good time. All we can do is enhance their efforts.

Yes, I readily admit that I still cut our bushes too much, but I do try to leave at least a couple of blooms on each bush for color in the garden. When these roses lose their petals, they're snapped or cut off at the neck. Because we are several miles from a paved road, there are no people passing by to admire them. But open blooms are colorful invitations to other visitors—butterflies and dragonflies, as well as hummingbirds every now and then. And always, we check carefully to see if a little tree frog has sought shade and moisture while nibbling on tiny insects between the petals. It is not unusual to find a pair who will stay tucked away in the same rose for a couple days. We've yet to detect any damage from their adventuresome ways between the petals.

Leaflets at Laterals

Close observation of roses will reveal various conditions that are seldom written about, one of which regards the leaflet that grows just below the joint of a lateral. It took me a long while to realize it, but these leaflets seem to come down with a case of blackspot far more readily than do regular leaflets on stems or canes. I've also noticed that, more times than not, these leaflets are naturally ready to drop. This is because that leaflet receives less nutrients due to the growth of the lateral that is much bigger and is taking most of the nutrients. Consequently, when time allows, it's a good idea to take off these leaflets before they become a host for blackspot.

In discussing this with Mel Bough, he said, "When I have time, just as a matter of course, I take those leaflets off." Then grinning, he added, "Needless to say, I don't always have time to do this."

Like most fungus diseases, blackspot is highly contagious. Look for a tell-tale black spot surrounded by a yellow patch. When even one part of a leaflet is affected, remove the entire leaf, because inevitably all of it is affected, even if the condition is not at first visible.

When cutting roses for the house or deadheading the bushes, I try to take off as many of these "leaflets at laterals" as possible—thinking that it's better to rid the bushes of vulnerable leaflets so that they don't infect the entire bush with blackspot. However, as Mel says, finding time to perform such preventive trimming is not easy.

Pull leaflets off to one side or the other, not down. Leaflets will snap off clean when pulled to the side; however, when pulled down they often tend to pull or peel the bark on the cane, inviting diseases and insects.

Naturally, not every would-be ailment can be noticed at one time, but in living with roses it pays to be a close observer. My grandfather said to me more than once (and he was not one who particularly believed in saying anything more than once or possibly twice) that it's easier to get into the habit of working with nature than against her—and a lot more rewarding. It's far easier and more satisfactory to take care of a beginning problem than an advanced one.

Blind Growth

New growth that produces stems and leaves, but no flowers, is spoken of as "blind" or "aborted" growth. What causes it? After researching the subject and talking to a lot of growers, both professionals and backyard rose growers, it seems that the most common reasons for blind growth are insect infestion, nutrient imbalance, and cold damage. The former culprit is usually the rose midge, a minute insect that literally devours the embryo of new growth, thus destroying any hope of a bloom bud. Second, as it can for other flowering plants, too much nitrogen can cause blind growth in roses, with the bush producing lots of leaves but few flowers. Finally, in temperate climates, a sudden cold snap can injure tiny, tender new growth to the point that it will not develop.

These three causes are just the most likely ones. Everyone we've talked to about blind growth agrees that the reasons for it are not fully understood, and many cite seasonal temperature changes as an additional contributing factor. Also, our own experience has been that the problem is more pronounced when a bush is not in a healthy state, and we have found that some varieties have a greater tendency to throw nonproductive growth than others. For instance, 'Fragrant Cloud' produces more than its share in our garden in certain seasons. So does 'Don Juan,' particularly in late winter or very early spring.

Because blind growth is usually weak and skinny, it is more apt to develop blackspot than foliage from master canes and limbs. Since it produces no blooms, you lose little by removing it as a preventive measure. Most growers agree that it does more good than harm to remove blind shoots, except when they are exceptionally strong and healthy. But there's always the nagging question of how many blind shoots to cut out. After all, the roses' leaves are its food factory, and without leaves the bush will literally starve.

My approach is to try to strike a happy medium. The smallest blind shoots get clipped off first, then about half the growth of the longer, heavier shoots. Look at the shoot carefully, then cut it off at the strongest point, just above a leaf. Thus pruned, blind growth will sometimes produce healthy, bloom-bearing laterals, but not always.

Disbudding

Disbudding is the process of removing all the flowerbuds in a spray except one, thus allowing all the strength of the cane to go into the single, remaining bud. The goal is to produce one large, full blossom, rather than a cluster of less-robust ones. I must confess to seldom taking part in this endeavor. It's not that I'm opposed to it, but rather that almost every time I notice a spray of buds that would lend itself to disbudding, I imagine how pretty the whole spray will be on the bush or in a vase. Then I think: I'll wait 'til the next budding, when almost inevitably the same scenario is repeated again.

Floribundas ideally lend themselves to the exercise of disbudding. They afford such grand masses of colors and forms that I keep thinking: there's no way to improve on them. Even when they're not flawless, there's so much to take pleasure in that imperfections take a back seat. Some Floribundas that have taken a front seat in our garden include: 'Sun Flare,' 'Bon-Bon,' 'Natalie,' 'Permanent Wave,' 'Angel Face,' 'French Lace,' 'Hannah Gordon,' 'Intrigue,' 'Diadem' and the striking 1998 AARS 'First Light.'

Fleeting flashes of little opalescent pearls…
Ahh… dainty dewdrops on my rose.

Compost is priceless. A generous covering of it in the rosebed not only feeds the bushes over long periods of time, it enhances elements in the soil, making them work more effectively and efficiently in supplying needed ingredients for healthy growth.

Compost can be bought commercially or it can be made free of charge in a small area in your own back yard. There are several ways to assure an ongoing supply of compost, one being to make an open bin of chicken wire. Into it, toss grass clippings, leaves, vegetable and fruit peels and greenery, coffee grounds and tea leaves, and other kitchen scraps. Don't add meat scraps or other animal products of any kind. And never, never add rose leaves or clippings, because they may carry disease or fungus spores that will thrive in the warm, moist atmosphere of the compost bin. Every once in a while, turn or stir the contents of the bin. If conditions are dry, add water every now and then. This is one of those projects that works constantly, every hour of every day, whether you're watching or not. Ideally, you should have two bins; that way, while the first one is "cooking," you can fill the second one. By the time it's full, the first one should be ready for use.

Another method for making compost is to place leaves in a bag, then tying it securely and stack the bags in any out-of-the-way spot. Depending upon the weather, the leaves will decompose in a matter of months and be ready to "do good"—and this without any help from those of us who tend the garden.

In our garden, and I suspect in others, mulch and compost seem to disappear overnight. This, of course, is not the case, but these materials do decompose rather rapidly, which is a good and healthy happening. Thus, it's also a good and healthy thing for the roses for the guardian of the garden to keep an ample supply readily available.

A fine potting soil can be made easily, by sifting compost through a wire screen. Nothing else is needed for seeds, seedlings, cuttings and as noted in the chapter on planting, for planting roses in open ground.

To make a great top-dressing for the rose bed, apply four to six inches of compost, then cover it with mulch. Very few weeds will find their way to the light of day through such a compost-mulch combination. A three- to four-inch layer will keep the soil and roots remarkably cooler, and at the same time retain valuable moisture.

Naturally, in adding a new rose to the garden, compost is a must to mix in with whatever else you are using in the planting process.

In our experience there is no substitute for mulch, which can be ground pine bark, ground wood of various kinds, pine needles (also called pine straw), grass cuttings (cured), eucalyptus mulch, melaleuca mulch, and of course, cypress mulch. There's no question that cypress makes a fine mulch; however, cypress stands are being devastated throughout Florida and in other regions where they grow, many being cut just to make mulch. It behooves gardeners and homeowners not to use it, and all consumers should discourage its sale for either commercial or home use. There are other mulches that are just as effective (and in most cases, less costly) and harvesting them is far less damaging to the environment.

Do not pile compost (or mulch) close around the main stalk or trunk of a bush. Leave a clear space of ten to twelve inches in all directions. This will allow the immediate soil around the bush to get its share of light and air, sun and rain, which the rose always needs.

My rosebuds... shredded like paper files!
How can this be?
Ah... now I see....
Wild turkeys having breakfast.

EPSOM SALTS

When asked "Why use Epsom salts?," almost all growers say—more or less—so there'll be more basal breaks, thus inducing maximum roses on sturdy canes. In layman's terms this means that the plant will branch more. How does it work? The active ingredient in Epsom salts is magnesium. In plant health and growth, the role of magnesium is quite extensive. It's found in the vital chlorophyll molecule and consequently it's directly associated with the successful utilization of sunlight by the plant in the process of manufacturing food. It is believed that magnesium is located in the "factories" of the plant cell where proteins are manufactured and where the sun's energy is used to put together the molecules of plant food.

Therefore, when Epsom salts is applied it is believed that the plant's ability to make protein is increased to the point that it operates at highest efficiency. All this makes it possible for the plant to produce a greater than average number of basal breaks.

The magnesium in Epsom salts does not alter the pH of the soil, and any excess that's not utilized by the rosebush is leached away to lower depths of soil by rain or watering. Even three or four applications per year pose no hazard to a rose bed that's nutritionally balanced.

In fact, many rose growers regularly schedule one application of Epsom salts every three months during the growing season, at the rate of one tablespoon per gallon of water. When applied dry, use one handful per bush, followed by generous watering.

I feed the roses...
And in return they feed my soul.

WHEN BUSHES LOOK UNHAPPY... WHAT TO DO?

All bushes do not respond alike to the same care. Even with regular watering and fertilization and adequate disease and pest control, inevitably a bush will appear unhappy—not wilted, necessarily, but not in a state of complete health and happiness. New growth may appear yellowish-green. Old foliage might have a dull papery look. Growth may be slow. How can you help?

First: Give water, lots of water.

Second: Apply two to three gallons of a reputable soluble fertilizer with high nitrogen such as Peters™ 20-20-20, MiracleGro™, or Bloomaster™. This will encourage the growth of new, healthy foliage.

Third: Stand back and wait.

You will probably be surprised at how soon the bush responds with greening foliage, followed by spurts of new growth—but don't stop! Keep watering, and repeat the soluble fertilizer feeding every week to ten days for about a month. In addition, a generous application of fish emulsion and/or cow manure will keep beneficial microorganisms in the soil hard at work. To encourage productive new growth, be sure to snip off small, twiggy growth and deadheads.

Discovering the source of your bush's discontent is the first step toward alleviating it. Countless growers advise soil testing. If you do not have your own means of analysis, take a sample to the nearest county Extension Office, or employ a reputable testing laboratory, many of which can be found through *American Rose* magazine.

Even if you aren't able to positively identify the cause of a problem, the rose may recover. A case in point is the rose 'Ave Maria.' Though officially classed as an orange pink, in our garden 'Ave Maria' has unfailingly been pure, intense, neon orange. This striking Hybrid Tea is a prolific bloomer that retains unfading color and remarkable form for days. She was a prize plant when purchased at Giles Rambling Roses in Okeechobee (now in Davenport) several years ago. Then, one fall day, for no apparent reason, she went into a quick state of apparent demise. After trying the usual remedies—cutting the bush back to lessen the load on its root system, using special sprays, examining roots on one side, et cetera—we decided there was nothing more we could do. Even so, I was reluctant to dispose of her, in part because I had been unable to find another bush on any rootstock, let alone 'Fortuniana.'

As is often the case, our attention went off in other directions. But one short cane remained green, and we let the bush remain in the garden. Along in mid-January we were replacing the mulch around the plants when we noticed a big, fat healthy basal on 'Ave Maria.' It just barely showed through the mulch and was a grand midwinter surprise. She has since sent up several more major basals, all straight, tall and strong (as is this rose's habit), and has been blooming prolifically for over a year. Once again I was reminded of a remark my grandfather made from time to time—that some things in nature are "unfiggeroutable"—and then, he'd always add, "in life, too, for that matter." To us, whether or not such a resurrection can be explained is not important. The fact that the rose is now healthy, happy and producing is enough.

I must confess that while there are those who pull out every bush that does not perform as a first-class rose, it's always been difficult for me to give up on a bush as long as there seemed any chance of saving it. I don't want people or plants to give up on me, so how can I do less in return? So we try everything that we can think of, all the while hoping to learn something that will help some distressed bushes live and be productive again, yet knowing that some won't.

If you believe in ridding the garden of everything not bright and beautiful, then you've missed some of the joy in seeing plants respond to love and care. On the other hand, by pulling out sickly plants you will save yourself some work and worry and make space for a brand-new, healthy bush—which brings its own kind of joy.

Floating flowers in the sky.
Or am I seeing butterflies?

Growing roses in containers can be highly successful, and particularly rewarding to those who do not have open space for bedded roses, or who have no space at all. A "garden" of roses in containers on an open porch, patio, balcony, the apron of a driveway, edge of a pool, or even on a rooftop can bring joy and beauty the year 'round in Florida as well as the warm months of the year elsewhere.

Roses are quite happy in containers providing the container is the right size and is placed in a location with ample sun. Otherwise, care is relatively the same as for roses planted in the ground, with the possible exception of water. Soil in pots is more exposed to light and heat, and therefore moisture evaporates more quickly. When temperatures are high, particularly on wind-blown days, containers must be checked often to see if soil has dried out, in which case, more water should be applied. At times when there is a run of hot, windy days, we water every day.

Containers come in so many materials, sizes and shapes that the selection can be boggling. However, there are some helpful guidelines.

For growing roses, there's probably nothing better than wood. It's a natural material, lightweight, and it's a very poor conductor of heat. Though durable, even if painted or sealed it will rot eventually. Before coming to Florida, I had some 200 roses—all sorts—in Charlotte, North Carolina, growing in bushel baskets sitting on the ground. To contain moisture, heavy mulch was piled almost to the rim of the baskets. Since the baskets were not solid they did not last very long, perhaps three or four years, but the bushes grew very large and were a mass of blooms from mid-May through October.

Nearly every year, October in Charlotte, North Carolina is the most spectacular time for roses. This particular year was no different, and it was early morning when the phone rang just as I was walking out the door. It was the president of the Charlotte Rose Society. It wasn't difficult to tell that something was wrong. He was in a panic! At that moment I had forgotten that it was the day of the local fall rose show. Because I had to leave town that morning, there was no way to even think of entering a bloom. Immediately, he said, "You *are*

coming? You *are* going to bring some blooms? For whatever reasons, not many have come this morning and we're afraid people will be disappointed…" and on and on he went.

At that point, I had to tell him I was on my way in another direction and could not possibly change plans. He sounded devastated, fearing that the show would not have the usual number of entries and the public would be sorely disappointed.

I had been out to the garden at first light and had seen dozens of splendid blooms, but the fact remained that I was firmly committed to be in Greensboro that morning. So I quickly told him the garden was in full bloom and they could have any and all of them if he could find someone to come and cut them. To this day I don't know who came to the garden, cut the roses, took them to the show, groomed, labeled and entered them—some three dozen blooms in all. But I do know that one splendid 'San Antonio,' an orange-red Grandiflora, won a blue ribbon, while several others won reds—all from a rose garden growing in bushel baskets.

Although we experimented with the same thing in Florida, we found that as year-round housing for roses, bushel baskets were even less longlasting in Florida's climate. That's when we started using wood and plastic containers.

Light-colored containers are the best choice; white or ivory-colored plastic is very good. Any dark-colored container (especially black) draws heat, which will burn feeder roots—or rot them, if soil is too wet. Red clay pots can also cause this reaction.

As to ideal size of containers, our experience has been that a container should be at least 20 inches wide and just as deep. We prefer the 24- by 24-inch size, but an 18- by 18-inch will afford satisfactory results for several years, especially for Miniatures, since they do not require as much space to excel.

Personally, we find that the less decorative a container is, the more pleasing the overall effect. We've never felt that a rose needs any extra enhancements.

We have several ivory-colored plastic containers that measure two feet wide and two feet deep and are slightly conical in shape, in which we planted

'Lady of Dawn' three years ago. The pots are placed about 10 inches deep in the ground to prevent their blowing over. A Floribunda, 'Lady of Dawn' is a huge grower with many long canes and large clusters of blooms. These container-grown bushes are very happy; they're actually a little larger than those of the same variety that were planted in the garden at the same time.

Feeding container-grown roses is not quite the same as feeding those in the ground. Their roots are more delicate and are more exposed to the elements. Roses in containers are also more subject to overfertilization and a build-up of mineral salts in the soil, so it's better to err on the side of underfertilizing. Don't worry—your roses will tell you if they're hungry. Three to four times annually, it's good to spread a handful of Epsom salts around each standard-sized container-grown bush. Frequently, but on no particular schedule, give your container-grown roses some "cow tea" and/or fish emulsion.

The care regimen for Miniature roses in pots is similar. We give our Minis very small amounts of granular fertilizer, but mostly they're fed soluble plant food: Bloomaster™, MiracleGro™ or Peters™ 20-20-20. Miniatures do very well on soluble fertilizer alone, but it must be applied consistently. For Minis, about a tablespoonful of Epsom salts every three to four months is ample, and regular applications of cow tea or fish emulsion are beneficial.

When potted roses (or other plants) are placed on the ground near trees or large shrubs, sooner or later there will be root intrusion through the holes into the containers. In our own garden, we had seven 20-gallon containers planted with Hybrid Teas and Floribundas. They grew and produced magnificently for the first two years. Several of the plants reached six feet in height and bloomed continually. However, not far into the third year we began to notice a gradual decline in the size of the bushes and the numbers of blooms. We immediately began to fertilize and water more, but the plants kept going downhill. Finally, thinking that maybe they were in too much shade, we attempted to move the pots.

We could not budge those containers! We had to literally dig around each one with a sharp-shooter spade to be able to move them. Right through the bottom holes there were pine and oak roots up to one-half inch in diameter growing up into those pots!

Considering the size of the intruding roots, we made no attempt to dig them out of the containers, and instead just cut them off. We then removed some soil at the edges of the containers and replaced it with a peat/cow manure mixture. After cutting back about one-third of each bush, granular and soluble fertilizers were applied, and then the bushes were watered heavily every day for several weeks.

In less than three weeks those plants produced at least six inches of new growth on every pruned cane, and in a week or two there were dozens of new buds. Some six weeks later, they were all blooming.

Upon reflection, it makes sense that all the food and water that's applied to roses attracts any nearby roots. The lesson learned was that a barrier of some sort, preferably wood or concrete, must be placed below the pot to keep roots from intruding into the bottom of the container.

Roses in pots are no more or less susceptible to bugs and blights than those in the ground, with the possible exception that nematodes are usually less of a problem. Control of pests and diseases in container-grown roses is exactly the same as it is for other roses. Close, regular inspection and a routine spray program are highly recommended.

Pale pink face of the fairest rose
reaching high in a delphinium sky...
Could it be she's trying to fly?

GROWING "SHOW" ROSES
by Doug Whitt

Doug Whitt, an ARS Consulting Rosarian (Life) has been living with and loving roses for some 40 years in various climates from Ohio to Atlanta to the present in Charlotte, North Carolina. His rose honors are enviable and include winning the Queen 24 times. A past president of the Charlotte Rose Society, Doug has been awarded the Society's bronze medal, as well as three ARS awards of merit for his writing. For 16 years he has written "Doug's Way with Roses" in Rosebud, *the society's newsletter, which has won ARS honorable mention for the past two years.*

Exhibiting roses adds a completely new dimension to the hobby of growing roses. To be a successful exhibitor, one must be more attuned to the finer details of rose excellence. This includes, but is not limited to, selecting exhibition varieties, building the rose beds, pest management, feeding, watering, knowledge of judging requirements, and interacting with other exhibitors.

The rose shows for a particular area of the country are usually scheduled to coincide with the average date of the peak of the first bloom cycle in the spring, or the last bloom cycle in the fall. Since it is a requirement that the entries be grown outdoors, this schedule is intended to take advantage of the more favorable climatic conditions for growing show quality blooms.

Once the date for a show has been established, the avid exhibitor can proceed with the extra duties required in producing competitive blooms. I'd like to qualify that statement with two observations. First, the necessary discipline of the exhibitor is *not* for all rosarians. Second, there is always a remote chance that a winning bloom may come from a garden that has not been well tended, particularly in the spring before the onset of inherent rose pests. The consistent award winner, though, will be the rosarian that tends to the finer details that produce superior blooms.

The actual point in time that the cycle of bloom has to begin in order to meet a target date should occur about six weeks prior to the show date. Most top exhibition hybrid tea roses cycle from the development of a bud at the leaf axil to the dropping of the sepals on the maturing flower bud in thirty-five to forty-five days. The real time of a complete cycle depends on variables that include the individual variety, the length of the cane

removed in pruning which involves the apical dominance of the primary bud remaining, daily weather conditions, et cetera.

To say the least, projecting the exact hour to prune for any show date is not an exact science. This uncertainty is the magic that whets our interest in exhibiting roses.

To force the beginning of the cycle requires the rosarian to make a pruning cut about one-fourth inch above a potential bud eye. These eyes are located at the junction of each leaf axil on a rose cane. The best potential blooms are produced by canes that are one year or less in age, and at least one-half inch in diameter. The exhibitor may even want to sacrifice some of the smaller canes so that the plant's energy can be directed to the ones that remain, producing larger, stronger, more competitive stem and bloom size.

To help compensate for some of the variables mentioned earlier, the advanced exhibitor will prune a different cane of a bush or of several bushes of a variety over the span of a week to ten days. This will result in maturing blooms over a longer period of time, regardless of the variables.

Now that the cycle has begun, the daily care and vigilance should be amplified. Exhibition quality roses are the finished product of a blend of the necessary nutrients and moisture, available to the plant in the correct soil pH of 6.2–6.8. I like to say that water is the magic ingredient in growing roses, for without it, nothing moves in the soil.

An application of a fertilizer to boost the bloom quality should be made after the pruning is completed at about six weeks prior to the show. This feeding should be high in phosphorus and potash, and the trace element zinc should be present, too. Chelated iron should be applied as a soil drench to assure dark green foliage. Magnesium sulfate (Epsom salts) will also help with the appearance of the foliage. Always when applying fertilizers, water before and after the application is made.

As the growth buds emerge and develop into canes, a watchful eye should be kept to intercept any pest that may visit the garden. Any side buds that form should be removed as soon as they are noticed, and only the dominant, center bud left to mature into a potential show bloom. The earlier the side buds are removed, the less the amount of unsightly scar tissue left to be distracting to the judge.

A weekly pest management program is a necessity to a successful exhibitor. The importance is evident when examining the list of nuisances that prey upon the species. Blackspot, while more prevalent in the fall, will on occasion invade the spring garden. Powdery mildew will often emerge in the cooler periods of the spring and fall. An array of insects can make their unwanted presence felt during the exhibition season. The smallest pest of all can be the most destructive if left unchecked, and that is the spider mite. All of these pests can be controlled by EPA-approved pesticides applied as instructed on the container labels, and on a systematic schedule throughout the growing season.

As the new growth progresses and the show date nears, it becomes important to zero in on the buds that have the greatest potential for show. It is more practical to focus on a few superior choices than the whole garden. It may be helpful in a large garden to use a note pad to record the finest of the lot so that none are overlooked.

Two weeks before the show, the plants that contain the canes selected for potential exhibition should be examined at least daily, more often if possible. This will intercept any unwanted pest before any irrevocable harm can be done. Any neighboring canes that are intruding on our potential show cane should be pruned to a lower level to lessen likely thorn damage to the foliage or bloom bud. Staking these potential Queens to prevent wind damage from abrasive action will reduce torn foliage and minimize injury to the flower bud.

At two weeks before the show, moisture in the soil is probably the most important ingredient to improve the bloom quality. Not a deluge of water that will leach all the nutrients past the feeder root system, but enough to assure that they are available in soluble form to meet the requirements of the maturing bloom buds. An application of a liquid food should be made now to each of the selected plants, and again it should be high in phosphorus and potash. To maintain the necessary soil moisture a gallon of water each day should be applied until the exhibition cane is cut.

Moisture in the soil is desirable, but moisture on the opening buds is a bane to exhibitors. Blustery, rainy days in the week or two prior to the show can impact the quality of the bloom, and rain will certainly reduce the potential of a specimen if permitted to fall directly into the opening bud. If sunlight shines on the buds for an extended period of time after their exposure to rainfall, the heat will cause blisters on the petals and discolor them enough to render them useless for exhibition. Moisture on the opening buds in the form of rainfall, heavy dew, the water sprinkler or from any overhead source is generally detrimental to the bloom quality.

To enhance the chances of having a winning entry despite unfavorable weather developments, some form of protection must be provided. No form of shelter is absolutely assured to withstand the violence of a thunderstorm short of growing roses in a greenhouse (but then they would be ineligible to win any awards at an ARS show), yet the avid exhibitor does not let a storm deter him from trying to protect a few blooms, come what may. Imagination and experimentation are beneficial in developing your own form of bloom protection. However, be prepared to explain to inquiring neighbors about the purpose of those mysterious gadgets hovering over certain blooms in the rose garden.

When providing bloom protection, keep in mind certain fundamental basics, and the cause and effect of the devices used. The rate of maturing growth and bud development decreases on cooler, cloudy days quite noticeably from the growth we see on warm sunny days. The complete shading of buds has the same effect in decreasing the rate of growth as clouds, and may be helpful at times if trying to slow the rate of development to meet a show date. Blooms covered and denied access to any direct sunlight will be paler than those exposed. Many varieties require direct sunlight to develop their beautiful contrasting colors ('Double Delight,' 'Color Magic,' 'Paradise,' etc.) and even in cloudy weather, do not reveal their beautiful contrasting colors. The fact is, the color in most varieties is enhanced by exposure to sunlight.

Now that color in the opening bud has begun to show, diligence is the name of the game. As the sepals drop, exposing the outside petals, removal of these guard petals may be necessary if they have white streaks. The earlier they are removed, the greater the chance the bloom will mature with perfect symmetry. Heat, moisture, insects, fungus diseases, wind, and other pests must be dealt with to produce a winner. Of these, insects and moisture will account for the major portion of concern. A daily misting of buds showing color using a one-quart hand sprayer containing an all purpose insecticide, to control thrips, will usually prevent the discoloration that often occurs if no protection is given.

Deciding when and at what time of day to begin cutting blooms for a show is a debatable issue. The sugar content of the opening bud is usually highest in the late afternoon, and is the preferred time for cutting. But a bud may reach the critical stage of opening in the morning, and if left on the plant until late afternoon for cutting would be worthless for exhibition. The general rule of thumb is to cut when the bud is ready, regardless of the time of day.

Refrigeration is almost a necessity to the consistently winning exhibitor. A refrigerator for roses increases the number of days that a potential blue ribbon winner can be held in storage and so increases the number of blooms available to choose from for entry into a show. There is a limit as to the length of time a bloom may be held before it begins to show its age, and a definite deterioration begins almost as soon as storage begins. Some entries resent any refrigeration at all as they will almost immediately lose color, or close tightly and refuse to open properly upon removal from the refrigerator. Blooms maturing over a long period of time in cooler weather will hold much longer than those maturing in hot weather. Heavy-petaled or many-petaled varieties will hold longer than those with fewer petals. The behavior of the various cultivars in your own garden will become known through trial and error as you exhibit them. The effect of the microclimates in your garden may require a relocation of some varieties to a site that receives more sun, while some will actually perform better with more shade, especially in the late afternoon.

Most success on the show bench will be enjoyed from specimens cut within three days of the show. Those cut the day prior to show time have a decided advantage as color is more brilliant and the substance or freshness is at its competitive best. Buds that must be cut early in the week of the show (the shows are usually on Saturday) must be cut at a tighter stage than if cut the day before the show. There comes a time when, if a bud is permitted to open too far on the plant, it will be past the desired two-thirds to three-quarters open state designated as the ideal stage in the "Guidelines for Judging Roses." It is better to cut the bud a little tight than to permit it to reach this "point of no return." A bud may be forced open with a little assistance, but cannot be closed again to the required position. Cutting the bud too tight is about as counterproductive as letting it open too far on the plant. The sepals (the green bud covering) must be down prior to removal from the plant or the bloom will not open at all.

Exhibition blooms should be cut with a stem length of at least eighteen inches and preferably a length of twenty-four inches. Don't cut them too short. You can always reduce the length if necessary, but it cannot be reattached once removed. Make the cuts on a slant, exposing more of the stem surface for greater water absorption. Place each stem into a pail of three or four inches of tepid water immediately upon removal from the plant. Put only two or three stems into each pail to prevent damage to the foliage. Identify each bloom with a small paper strip placed around the stem just under the bud. Store in a cool, dark room for an hour or so, conditioning the blooms while the water cools to room temperature.

I recommend that each stem be groomed before placing in the refrigerated area for storage until the day of the show. Using clear water, mist the foliage lightly (use the sink for a work area) and dab dry with a quality paper towel cut into six inch squares (do not get moisture on the bloom bud). Inspect for foliage damage and trim if required. Use large vases or one-quart plastic milk jugs with the top removed to store the groomed roses in the cooler. Place three or four inches of water (preferably with a floral preservative added) into each container, and place a plastic sandwich bag over the bloom to minimize moisture loss from the petals.

The morning of the show, these exhibition blooms can be transported in buckets or containers with fresh water, and should be kept cool during the trip. The necessary show schedule entry tags and display vases will be available at the show.

Good luck!!

There's nothing as good for the soul
As You… and a rose.

Growing Roses with…
TIM MYERS

Orban's Nursery, Inc. at Bradenton has accomplished much for rose growers since the early 1990s. Co-owned by Tim Myers and Martin Orban, the nursery is primarily a wholesale operation. However, twice a year it welcomes interested groups to the nursery by appointment. Three days a week, fall through spring, Orban's roses are offered to the public at Crowder Bros. Ace Hardware in Bradenton, Florida.

Tim Myers says many people ask him What is a "patent" rose? His answer: "Rose breeding is an expensive business. Each year millions of crosses are made in an effort to produce the 'perfect rose.' If a breeder is successful and can prove he has something new or better, he is granted a patent and then is allowed to collect a royalty from anyone who wishes to grow his rose. This royalty may be collected for up to 17 years. The price difference between a patent and non-patent rose is this royalty."

There are over 50 recognized rose hybridizers in the world. These are the breeders who develop new varieties by cross-pollinating one rose with another. Countless crosses are made every year in an effort to produce a rose worthy of being named an All-America Rose Selection.

To this writing only one amateur rose hybridizer, a pipe fitter in Cincinnati, has ever won the coveted AARS award. It was in 1972, when Carl Meyer's 'Portrait' was chosen. From the birth of the first cross to its debut, it took eleven years for his prize to make it to the top of rosedom. About his rose, Carl Meyer says 'Portrait,' a deep rose-pink Hybrid Tea, is amazingly free of disease, particularly black spot, and that the bush is extremely hardy. 'Portrait' is a classic rose-colored rose, neither true pink, nor red, somewhat the color of 'Perfume Delight.' The bud is long and tapered, the bush shapely. It blooms prolifically and is an excellent cut rose.

We grew 'Portrait' in North Carolina and have grown it here in Florida also, but have not been able to find a bush in recent years. Although new roses being developed every year traditionally push older varieties into the background, we can hope that interest in 'Portrait' might be resurrected one fine day so that a grower somewhere might start producing it.

"From our experience here at Orban's," Tim says, "We have found that after quality rose bushes have been purchased, roses require three basic things for successful, happy growing that produces big, beautiful blooms: Water, full sunshine, and regular fertilization. Finally, if you are having a problem with growing roses, wherever you are, help is as near as the telephone or fax, a reliable dealer, members of the nearest rose society, or a Consulting Rosarian of the American Rose Society… and, a book such as you are reading now. Growing roses is like any other pursuit in that all it takes is the dedicated desire to succeed."

PERFECT AND NOT-SO-PERFECT

So many times, I think: As human beings we are so far from perfection ourselves that we shudder at the thought of friends giving up on us or expecting the utmost from us. So how can we give up on roses that fall a little short, as we too often do?

This is not a declaration of right or wrong. This is only to point out that some who grow roses want perfection, absolute. Further, these growers will not tolerate the too-small bloom, a blemished petal, a short stem, or a form that's even a little out of kilter. While we admire these growers for their pursuit of perfection, we are not growing roses in a perfect garden. We love them all, with or without blemishes, with or without warts. A bud or bloom with a three-inch stem ends up in a tiny bottle on the sink shelf, no less admired for its lack of a long stem.

This does not imply that we do not strive for that perfection of bud and bloom and bush. While we can't claim to have had perfection every day, we probably have had more than we deserve. And while it may read like an excuse or perhaps to justify our falling short of growing superlative roses each and every day, often there is the thought that perhaps not unlike beauty itself, perfection is in the eye of the beholder.

The first photo I saw of 'Ballerina' was in Park Seed Company/Wayside Gardens catalog, Hodges, South Carolina. The entire bush was awash with hundreds of small five-petal strawberry pink blooms with white eyes—dozens of long, full clusters at the ends of dozens of canes all growing from the central crown of the bush at ground level. It truly looked like a perfect pink fountain, reminiscent of April's weeping pink cherry trees in the red hills of Virginia whose dozens of weeping limbs emerge from a central point at the top of the trunk. Like the rose, each limb is host to dozens of pink cluster blooms on

'Ballerina' Hybrid Musk
(photo courtesy Wayside Gardens)

graceful, arching arms in almost perfect symmetry.

Although knowing it was not on 'Fortuniana' rootstock—since Park/Wayside sells roses only on 'Dr. Huey' understock, or own rootstock roses—I could not resist what I thought would be an extraordinary addition to our garden, reasoning that after all, some 'Dr. Huey' understock bushes do very well here. Right then, an order was sent out for 'Ballerina.'

After being planted in January, she grew quickly into a handsome bush, bloomed sparingly but beautifully that first spring. In the following months of that whole year there was not one repeat bloom! However, the bush was large, its fountain-shape was superb and its small leaves were a vibrant, healthy green.

The next spring, there were a few canes with small clusters of blooms but very few. However, color and form were excellent.

Since it was a large bush, and knowing how we always seem to need space for another bush, we considered taking it out. But then the thought: let's give it one more year. So the next January it was pruned severely. The bush responded immediately with lush new growth, and in about six weeks, it bloomed a bit more but nothing like the catalog photo.

Again the dilemma: take it out, or keep it? Since at that moment we did not have another bush to plant in its place, we ignored it and left it be.

'Ballerina' paid no attention to summer's coming nor going. Now it is late September. The bush has continued to grow rapidly with long graceful canes in every direction and October is within hollerin' distance. Seemingly, almost overnight, several of those long arching canes are in glorious full bloom! And somehow, I had not even noticed the little buds coming on. But then, when looking more carefully, it was easy to see many more embryo buds emerging. No, it still is not a "pink fountain" with hundreds of blooms as shown in the catalog, but oh, this display of fall bloom has proved its worth—earning 'Ballerina' a permanent spot in the garden.

This far south in Florida (Glades County/ USDA zones 9–10), maybe 'Ballerina' is a little like Samuel Johnson's dog who only had three legs: the wonder wasn't that the little animal didn't run well, but that he ran at all!

'Ballerina' is not perfect and does not bloom prolifically, but she is a beauty with a unique Victorian charm and grace all her own. She is welcome in our world.

We're still trying to find a bush on 'Fortuniana,' which just may be what she needs to be "born again" and become a real Southerner, showing off that perfect pink fountain that we first fell in love with in the catalog, as well as showing off her rating of 8.8 from the 2001 *Handbook for Selecting Roses*.

As Scarlett said, "Tomorrow is another day"— which just may be the tomorrow all our roses will be perfect.

And the rose whispered:
My imperfections are many
but I love you just the same.

Growing Roses With...
MEL AND RITA BOUGH

Mel and Rita Bough, who live on Holly Road in Fort Myers, Florida, are nationally-accredited ARS Life Judges. (The designation of a "Life Judge" by the ARS is no longer made.) They are also ARS Consulting Rosarians.

Mel has been Chairman over the Deep South District Consulting Rosarians, which is comprised of Georgia, Alabama, and Florida.

"The longer I grow roses the more I tend to keep the growing procedures as simple as possible. Upon first starting out, most people seem to go overboard on almost everything, which includes whatever they read as well as what different growers—both new and seasoned growers—say to do or not to do, and the first thing you know they get messed up. And I include myself in this group!

"I don't know why, but it seems at first, we who are dedicated to growing roses think that everything we read is gospel, which is not necessarily true.

"After twenty-some years of growing roses in Fort Myers, I'm convinced that it's best for the average grower to stay with a simple spray program, along with ample fertilizer and water. Naturally, for best results, the rose bush itself must be of good quality.

"I've found that a lot of rose growers tend to turn would-be rose growers off by taking the stand of making growing them so complicated that it discourages many people. If it's too involved and too time-consuming a lot of would-be growers are not going to plant the first rose.

"I feel that those who want to start growing roses should know and understand, before they plant the first bush, that roses do need routine, consistent care, but it does not have to be an all-consuming chore.

"There was a time when I spent nearly every spare hour tending our roses. Now I don't do that, and they seem to do just as well as when I had the time to constantly tend them.

"The average home gardener—even one who has a considerable number of roses, a hundred or even more—doesn't necessarily have to follow all the same rules that a commercial grower does. You can easily and satisfactorily get by with a lot less.

"For instance, I spray for insects only when I see that we have an insect problem. In other words I do not routinely spray an insecticide—fact is, I hardly ever use insecticides. I think it depends upon the quality bloom you want. If it's absolute perfection you're aiming for, then you'll probably need to use an insecticide of one type or another depending upon the insect you're trying to control. This is not the case with fungicides. I regularly spray for control of fungus diseases.

"The basic difference is whether you're growing roses for home enjoyment for yourself or others, or growing them competitively for shows. A little blemish here and there won't generally spoil the beauty and enjoyment of a rose in the home. However if you're growing roses for shows, it goes without saying that they must be as nearly perfect as possible."

A bright new day in the garden:
the sound of roses—silent songs of how I feel.

What does it really mean to grow roses purely organically? It means that no chemicals will be used in planting or caring for them. Only natural ingredients and materials will be used.

In the planting, follow the directions for size of hole, removing all the soil. Then mix together about one-third each existing soil, sphagnum peat moss, and manure, either dehydrated or natural pasture. It is good to add homemade compost or commercial compost to the mix, and the addition of top soil or natural leaf or peat mold from the woods is also very good. If your existing soil is nothing but hard, lumpy clay, discard it and substitute a mixture of sharp sand and compost. Then, follow the directions on page 53 for the planting and watering, leaving out the superphosphate but including bone meal, which is organic.

When feeding roses organically, remember that organic fertilizers—natural manure, humus, compost, almost any decomposed matter—take much longer to get into the plant's system and start nourishing it than do chemical fertilizers. Consequently, in order for roses to be supplied the nutrients they must have for vigorous growth and beautiful blooms, natural fertilizer must be applied often and regularly. Manure tea (or fish emulsion), should be applied at least every three to four weeks in generous quantities. Manure tea is manure mixed with water that has been allowed to steep for several days. This manure tea does not, however, take the place of solid applications of manure, which also should be applied in generous amounts every three to four weeks.

What type of manure should you use? Most full-line garden centers stock dehydrated cow, sheep and chicken manures, as well as Milorganite™, a dehydrated product derived from sewage sludge. We use natural manures, including horse when we can get it, but mostly—because it's readily available to us—pasture manure variously known as "meadow muffins" or "cow cakes." Other all-natural, organic plant foods include ocean kelp meal, alfalfa meal, and Ebb-Tide Greensand™. Some rose growers alternate plant foods and others don't. If we have a product on hand that we know is good

for roses, we use it. If we acquire a different product that we know is equally good, without a second thought we use it. We are not organic purists; we find that a common-sense combination of natural products and chemical materials gives us the best results.

Rich compost can be easily made from anything in nature that decomposes: leaves (but never rose leaves because of the risk of spreading disease), grass clippings, vegetable and fruit peelings, straw, coffee grounds, tea leaves, et cetera. Add compost to the soil when planting a new rosebush or use it as a top-dressing around established plants.

Growing roses organically is not difficult but don't expect quick results. Once the bushes start responding to organic feedings they'll keep on responding as long as they get enough of what they need. Compost, humus, peat moss, manure—all mixed in to the soil—allow an excellent gas exchange so the soil has enough oxygen to support the microorganisms that convert nutrients into food forms available to the plants.

As the Rosarian Rambler, Howard Walters writes, "Humus is the key to good rose growing, holding and making available water and nutrients, increasing porosity of the soil and supporting the 'living' process."

Nearly all soil that's used over and over needs organic matter to make it "come alive" again. Digging out soil and entirely replacing it is a time-consuming and expensive undertaking. However, "tired" soil can be rejuvenated by adding ample humus—lots of manure—with water, water, water. No rose food, organic or inorganic, can do its work without water. Before applying any type of fertilizer, thoroughly water the bushes. First water, then apply the food, then water again.

Is there such a thing as organic spray? Yes, a limited number of these materials exists, and more are being developed all the time. One of the best known is Green Light Rose Defense™, which captures the fungicidal, miticidal and insecticidal properties of neem. Rose Defense™ was originally marketed as Triact™, a product for the commercial greenhouse industry, but it is now available to consumers nationwide. It is a hydrophobic extract from the seeds of the neem tree, processed and formulated to retain fungicidal and miticidal activity. It can be used to control major diseases and pests on roses, as well as on common landscape trees and shrubs. In USDA and university trials, Rose Defense™ has been found to control such diseases as blackspot, powdery mildew, rusts and anthracnose, as well as common insect pests such as two-spotted mites, aphids, mealy bugs and scales.

We have been using Rose Defense™, in combination with commercial fungicides, since 1996. It has definitely allowed us to reduce our frequency of spraying. Time was when we sprayed every 7 to 8 days, but now, providing the bushes look healthy and disease-free, we spray every 8 to 12 days. However, if we see any sign of a disease or insect in the interim, we immediately treat it.

Although we are not organic growers in the strict sense, we rarely use insecticides except to "spot spray" an intolerable infestation of aphids, spider mites or other insects—an intolerable infestation being one that cannot be washed (or picked) off. We always try the water method first, thinking we have everything to gain and nothing to lose. The water is good for the roses and most of the time will get rid of at least some of the bugs. When conditions are right for spider mites, they will return, usually when the weather is hot and dry. They love roses, too. If they reappear, grab the hose and start washing.

An organic product that's recommended for the control of worms (caterpillars, corn ear and others) is Thuricide™, a liquid. The wettable powder form of Thuricide™ is called Dipel™. These products offer biological control in the form of Bt, *Bacillus thuringiensis*. Neither Thuricide™ nor Dipel™ harms beneficial insects. Thus the cherished lady bug is safe to devour as many aphids as she can hold!

On wings of a silent daybreak…
the pure, sweet scent of roses.

NEW DEVELOPMENTS IN ORGANIC GARDENING
by Gene McAvoy, UF/IFAS Extension Agent, Hendry County

Many rose gardeners choose to avoid chemicals out of concern for health and environment. Effective management of bugs and maladies through natural biorational means can be uncomplicated if certain rudimentary principles are observed.

An ecologically sound approach to pest and disease control is integrated pest management or IPM. Whereas chemical solutions focus on eradicating pests and diseases with toxic compounds, IPM incorporates different strategies.

Astute gardeners realize that pest and disease control begins before the rose is planted. Healthy, vigorous plants are their own best defense against pests and diseases. It is important that plants be kept strong and healthy by building healthy soils with compost, manure and organic fertilizers which improve soil by providing essential plant nutrients.

Many techniques help frustrate pests and diseases. Site selection is fundamental. Roses growing in adverse conditions invite problems. Good drainage is a must as is adequate sunshine. Choose a site where air circulates freely. In warm climates grow varieties grafted onto nematode-resistant *Rosa fortuniana*.

To successfully fight pests and diseases, you must recognize problems. Learn the life cycles of common pests and diseases so you can anticipate potential problems. Blackspot, for instance, will be a bigger problem during warm, rainy weather than when conditions are cool and dry.

While learning about rose pests and diseases, learn about and protect beneficial organisms that can help maintain roses in a healthy state. Fewer than one percent of insects are harmful and many are actually helpful. There are many beneficial insects—lady beetles, lacewings and others—that are voracious insect predators and will help control aphids, whiteflies and other soft bodied insects.

Monitor health of bushes frequently. Early detection is key to successful pest/disease control. Many problems can be literally nipped in the bud if detected early by hand-picking or pruning affected foliage. Remember to disinfect pruners as some diseases are spread from plant to plant by contaminated equipment.

Learn to tolerate a few insects and an acceptable level of damage. Attempting to maintain roses totally pest and disease free is not only impractical but wastes time and money. Healthy roses will do well even after losing a few leaves or blossoms to pests. But what if pests or diseases reach unacceptable levels? Don't despair. There are very effective biorational controls available to help tip the ecological balance back in favor of your prize roses. For instance: copper and sulfur are natural fungicides that help prevent and control blackspot and powdery mildew. Neem oil and fungicidal soaps are effective against some fungal diseases. Some gardeners use baking soda while others swear by tomato leaf tea for blackspot, which is concocted by grinding a handful of tomato leaves in three pints of water and applied as a foliar spray. Also, plain water is effective in discouraging aphids and mites when sprayed in a strong stream from a hose.

Soap and oil sprays are nontoxic standbys that are effective against many insects. Since both act by interfering with an insect's breathing, thorough coverage is critical. For persistent problems, rotenone and pyrethrum are powerful natural insecticides.

Neem is a relatively new, environmentally-friendly insect control product. Neem and neem oil are two distinct products. Neem is the common name for azadirachtin, a chemical extracted from the neem tree. Neem oil is a byproduct of the extraction process. Azadirachtin is not really an insecticide, but rather an antifeedant which renders plants unpalatable to pests, as well as a growth regulator which prevents insects from maturing. Neem tree oil is an insecticidal oil with fungistatic properties.

Scientists have identified several disease organisms that infect pests which attack roses. One is a class of products known as Bts, short for *Bacillus thuringiensis,* that sickens and kills only caterpillars.

Related *Bacillus popillae,* known as milky spore disease, is effective against Japanese beetle larvae but is selective and harmful only to target pests. Other biocontrol agents that have been discovered include viruses which control insects, as well as beneficial bacteria and fungi that colonize plant roots and protect them from diseases. Many are commercially available and should come into wider use as better understanding of their effective application strategies is developed.

A new class of green fungicides, strobulurins, has recently become available. Derived from natural forest fungi, these are safe for use around people and pests, posing little threat to the environment while controlling a broad spectrum of diseases. Perhaps the most exciting development is the discovery of immune-like systems in plants and naturally occurring proteins which turn these systems on and off. Until recently it was thought that only animals had immune systems. Research at Cornell University and elsewhere has led to the discovery of systemic acquired immunity in plants. It's now evident that plants can react to infections by responding to potential attackers by releasing toxic compounds that inhibit or kill invading organisms. Application of certain proteins to plants can turn on a plant's natural immune system in advance of a disease attack, greatly increasing its chances of fighting off the pathogen.

Although science will never substitute for a dedicated gardener's green thumb and the gentle art of gardening, it is comforting to know that it has provided us with a number of environmentally sound pest and disease control options.

Now pale and frail, petals drift softly on the wind...
Back to Earth from whence they came.

ARS CONSULTING ROSARIANS – A VALUABLE RESOURCE
by Steve Jones, ARS National Consulting Rosarian Program Chair

There are many misconceptions of what Consulting Rosarians (CR) are and what is expected of them. This is not just another honor to earn or a certificate to hang on the wall and then do nothing. CRs are the backbone of the American Rose Society (ARS), and they are expected to help with the goals of the society. Participating is the main element of being a CR, and all CRs are expected to participate.

I have yet to meet a rose grower who was not eager to help another grower or would-be grower. It seems that roses bring out the best qualities of generosity and helpfulness in people. In addition to the information you receive from your local nurserymen and rose-growing friends and acquaintances, advice and assistance are always at hand by contacting an ARS Consulting Rosarian. These wonderful people are knowledgeable and enthusiastic, dedicated to helping those who have questions or problems in their own gardens—and they provide this service without price or obligation.

The mission of the Consulting Rosarian program is "To enthusiastically inspire a love and appreciation of roses, to stimulate new memberships, serve the membership, be knowledgeable of all aspects of rose culture, and share that knowledge with others."

Becoming a Consulting Rosarian of the American Rose Society is not an easy task—but oh, what an accomplishment, and with such grand rewards for those who love and revere roses, beginners or seasoned growers alike.

Here are the qualifications and responsibilities required of a Consulting Rosarian, provided courtesy of the American Rose Society.

Any member of the American Rose Society may qualify as a Consulting Rosarian by the following:

1. Must be a member, either regular or associate, of the American Rose Society for three consecutive years.
2. Must be an active member of a local rose society.
3. Must have grown roses of various types for at least five years and should be knowledgeable in all equipment and materials related to rose culture.
4. Must provide three letters of recommendation by any three Consulting Rosarians on the form provided by the District Consulting Rosarian Chairman.
5. Must attend an ARS school/workshop for Consulting Rosarians and complete an open-book examination based on the material contained in this manual.
6. Must know and be willing to live up to the Consulting Rosarian Guide.
7. Must be willing to attend no less than one Consulting Rosarian School every three years.
8. Must submit an annual completed individual report form to the District Chairman of Consulting Rosarians by the date designated by the District Director.
9. Must exhibit a continuing willingness to share knowledge and an enthusiasm for the rose and the American Rose Society.

Active Consulting Rosarians

In order to remain as an "active" Consulting Rosarian, one must attend a Consulting Rosarian School once every three years.

Consulting Rosarian Code

Every Consulting Rosarian, on accepting the appointment, should be fully cognizant of the Consulting Rosarian Code and should wholeheartedly be willing to live up to the code:

"I, [NAME], accept the honor of the official appointment as a Consulting Rosarian of the American Rose Society for the [DISTRICT NAME] District. I pledge my earnest efforts toward the increase and stimulation of membership in the American Rose Society, in cooperation with the District Director. I shall uphold the highest standards of our American Rose Society in inspiring a love and appreciation of roses, their culture and exhibition. The aims and purposes of the American Rose Society shall be foremost in my mind in pro-

BETTY LOU DICKEY
in Praise of...
Genuine Consulting Rosarians

"Once, many years ago, there was a little North Carolina girl whose summer pastime was making corsages from flowers and ferns, even arborvitae 'borrowed' from all the neighbors' gardens. The little girl's mother said these creations looked like funeral flowers, but that did not deter the childish determination that someday she would grow her own posies.

"Finally at age 60, having acquired four acres of land, the now-big girl met Arlan Hale, a retired chemist who was growing beautiful roses down the road in LaBelle, Florida. He introduced me to the joys and disappointments of having one's own rose garden, sharing his time and knowledge as a rosarian. Under his tutelage, I planted 75 rose bushes. Mr. Hale not only gave me great and lengthy advice but also his special fertilizer and oftimes his own rose bouquets.

"It was not long before my 'rose man' became ill, and as a result so did many of my bushes, as he was no longer able to help me.

"I received suggestions for diagnosis and treatment for my problems from numerous sources, but they were not effective. I sadly destroyed 13 of my plants and was certain that the remaining roses would soon meet the same fate. Then a friend put me in touch with the Richards, Eula and Carroll, of North Fort Myers, Florida, who are ARS Consulting Rosarians and who have been truly dedicated rosarians for many years. They have over 200 rosebushes in their garden. Eula is a national rose show judge who conducts seminars and travels widely in the interest of roses. Carroll grafts and grows, does the planting, weeding and spraying!

"I called these dear folks one day and they came out to my garden the very next day to examine my rosebushes and recommend treatment for the troubles I was having. Since that time two years ago, Eula and Carroll became my mentors and my professional advisors. They taught me so much and gave me so much, not only of their advice but of their time, new plants, their chemicals, cut flowers—as well as all the iced tea I could drink!

"After five years I am still a novice at growing roses. I no longer make corsages, but I love the pleasure, the therapy, and the challenges involved in caring for my roses. The blossoms are sometimes great, sometimes not so great; nevertheless, I am hooked on growing roses thanks to Arlan Hale and Eula and Carroll Richards, who are honest-to-gosh rosarians. I shall ever be grateful to them for their kindness and help, which has enabled me to share my flowers with my church and friends.

"According to Eula, the 'price' I must pay for these gifts in my garden is to help others who grow roses whenever I can."

Twilight in the garden—all is still
Except for sounds of petals falling.

moting and forming new rose societies, securing new members, and serving present members and anyone interested in roses. I recognize and accept the responsibilities of this post, as well as the privilege of service."

The Consulting Rosarian Guide

It is incumbent upon every Consulting Rosarian to exercise every effort to further a greater interest in the rose. They should SHARE their knowledge with those less informed on the care of roses.

The Consulting Rosarian should not WAIT to be asked but should share knowledge voluntarily and willingly help others. They should be available to help friends, neighbors and rose society members in any way possible. In fact, they should be willing to help anyone who is interested in learning about roses and their culture.

Being a Consulting Rosarian is more than an obligation to share technical knowledge concerning roses. It involves participation in every aspect of the rose society to which they belong, be it helping set up a rose show, showing slides at meetings, writing articles for news media or publications or serving on any of the society's committees. The object is to HELP others and to stimulate greater interest in growing roses and further the scope of this growth and scope of the rose society to which they belong. On the broader level, Consulting Rosarians should be ever active in furthering the cause and interests of the American Rose Society in whatever way they can. Here are some of the things a Consulting Rosarian should do:

IN THEIR OWN GARDENS: The most obvious obligation is to grow good roses, to grow a variety of roses to include Hybrid Teas, Floribundas, Grandifloras, Climbers, Miniatures, Tree Roses, Shrubs and Old Garden Roses. There is no need to have acres of each, but there should be a few of each. The roses in the garden should include the most popular of the new introductions, to be informed and better able to answer questions concerning them.

Consulting Rosarians should be acquainted with everything in rose culture, be it a new type of sprayer, a new insecticide or fungicide. They should

be familiar with state and federal laws and regulations pertaining to use of chemicals in the garden. They should know how the garden chemicals should be used, safety precautions to follow, et cetera.

The rose garden of any Consulting Rosarian should be open for all to enjoy and admire and the roses should be of the quality to inspire and encourage others to grow roses.

The Consulting Rosarian should be familiar with chemical and nontoxic approaches to rose growing. Regardless of the approach Consulting Rosarians take in their own garden, chemical, no chemicals or Integrated Pest Management, it is important to be knowledgeable about all approaches.

IN THE LOCAL ROSE SOCIETY: Consulting Rosarians should not have to be asked to help. They should meet with other Consulting Rosarians to share knowledge and information. They should volunteer to help wherever and whenever needed. They should be willing to hold an office, serve on the board of directors, head a committee or perform any other task which will further the interest in the society.

Consulting Rosarians should let it be known they are willing to help members any way they can. Special attention should be given to helping new members with rose information. Consulting Rosarians should be willing to open their gardens to others.

IN THE AMERICAN ROSE SOCIETY:
1. Assist members and non-members with cultural problems.
2. Obtain new members for the American Rose Society.
3. Work together in organizing and assisting new rose societies.
4. Encourage each organized rose group to sponsor at least one rose show per year.
5. See that district and national shows do not conflict and whenever possible, that local shows do not conflict with any other show.
6. Attend the Consulting Rosarian Meeting each year at the district meeting.
7. Be a member of the district Public Rose Garden Committee where one exists.

8. Complete and submit the annual Roses in Review survey each year, and the Triennial Survey every three years.
9. Be in attendance at the local rose shows, answering all questions.
10. Maintain an American Rose Society Membership Booth at all local rose shows.

A willingness to share knowledge and an enthusiasm for the joys of growing roses are the identifying traits of a good Consulting Rosarian. He/she must be willing to give of himself and have time to help others—members and non-members alike.

A good Consulting Rosarian must, in addition, keep the aims and ideals of the American Rose Society ever in mind and must be dedicated to furthering those aims and ideals.

Finally, a good Consulting Rosarian must convey to others that growing roses is a hobby with a tremendous potential for enjoyment and satisfaction that is greatly increased by sharing knowledge and love of the rose with all.

It is against the principles of the Consulting Rosarian program to charge a fee for rose advice.

Steve Jones lives and grows roses in Valencia, California. For a list of Consulting Rosarians in your area, check the ARS website (www.ars.org) or call ARS at (318)938-5402.

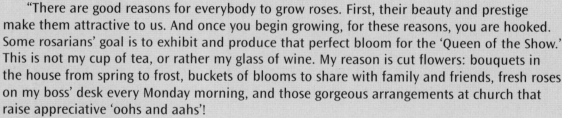

Growing Roses With...
ISABELLE DE SERCEY

"There are good reasons for everybody to grow roses. First, their beauty and prestige make them attractive to us. And once you begin growing, for these reasons, you are hooked. Some rosarians' goal is to exhibit and produce that perfect bloom for the 'Queen of the Show.' This is not my cup of tea, or rather my glass of wine. My reason is cut flowers: bouquets in the house from spring to frost, buckets of blooms to share with family and friends, fresh roses on my boss' desk every Monday morning, and those gorgeous arrangements at church that raise appreciative 'oohs and aahs'!

"Whatever the excuse, growing roses is a rewarding hobby, but like that swimming pool next door, that beautiful expanse of crystal clear water rippling in the sun, it does not just happen. It takes money, time and *savoir faire* to keep that pH in balance and the pests and fungi at bay.

"Roses in my area of North Florida will bloom from mid-March to frost, and only roses will do that. The best time to decide about a rose garden is to visit others' gardens in the fall. Bushes and blooms might not be at their peak, but they will give you an idea of which ones survived the heat of the summer, the rainy season and possibly hurricane winds. When you have a list of your favorites, cut it in half. Start small. It is easier to expand than to cut down. You can trust me on this!

"The second best advice is to join your local rose society. Not only are rosarians a wonderful group of people, but they will tell you all you need to know about rose culture for your region and climate."

*I don't know whether nice people tend to grow roses,
or growing roses makes people nice.*
—*Roland A. Browne, b. 1939, American professor*

4. Manifold Blessings

THE JOYS OF GIVING ROSES

In the eyes and gardens of those who have lived with them, roses give far more than they receive. As one poet wrote: "Roses are Earth's music from the heart of God."

The magnetism, the mystery, and the romance of roses has endured for centuries. Now, more than ever, with the world's most renowned flower being grown all over the world, that romance and mystery has escalated to new heights of admiration and adoration.

As sepals fall and petals begin to unfurl, the magnetic attraction of roses increases hour to hour. It is a phenomenon that is difficult, if not impossible, to explain. But at the very root, the very heart, of the drama is the inexplicable joy and love for this flower that has been around for some 35 million years. It is a love and affection that lasts a lifetime, both in the growing and giving of roses.

When to Cut Roses

As cut flowers, roses will last longer, will retain more stamina, and will have truer colors if they are cut in early morning. The next best time is evening. Do not cut roses from mid-morning to mid-afternoon. Since I'm a dedicated rose grower and not a scientist, I cannot prove this, but I've been told by professionals and have read in various respected rose journals that roses wilt when cut at midday because the sugar level and water in the blooms and bushes are lowest at that time, whereas they are highest in early morning and next-highest in late day or early evening. Also, quite naturally, the higher heat of midday takes its toll. In practice this has been proven countless times in our own garden. Some growers vow that early evening is best for cutting. Others prefer early morning, which is our favored time. Not only is the garden itself awaken-

ing, so is our world, and when buds are cut early, the wonder and beauty of their opening stages can be enjoyed all day.

If at all possible, water your roses at least thirty minutes before cutting, or even the night before, especially in the summertime. You'll be delighted with the added aura of freshness they will exhibit—some, of course, more than others.

For maximum longevity of cut roses, take a container of room-temperature water with you to the garden. Upon cutting the stem, immediately immerse it in water. Never use cold water for cut roses. Lukewarm to very warm will allow the cut stem to absorb more water more quickly.

Do not arrange cut roses before "conditioning" them. First, recut their stems under water. This simple step allows the rose to "drink" a maximum amount of water. Hold the end of the stem under water while making a fresh cut; this prevents air from getting to the cut. Then remove all the leaves that will be under water in the vase. Rinse the remaining foliage to remove any residue from sprays, dust or anything else that might be on it. Contaminants tend to enhance bacterial growth which will shorten vase life. Place the roses in a container of warm water and put them in a refrigerator for several hours or overnight.

Where to Cut Stems

"How do you know where to cut the stem of a rose?" That old rule-of-thumb advice, "Cut just below the first five-leaflet" is good to a point. However, some highly-respected growers have found that to unerringly go by this rule is not necessarily best for the bush. There is probably no rule that could apply to all bushes, since each and every one is different.

For example, if one faithfully applied the "five-leaflet" rule to bushes that almost always produce very long stems, these particular bushes could quickly get out of hand by growing too tall and spindly. Examples of these include 'Gold Medal,' 'Hannah Gordon,' 'Lagerfield,' 'Permanent Wave,' 'Lady of the Dawn' and in our garden, even that very old, very precious 'Cécile Brünner,' which grows larger—as well as taller and wider—here than anywhere we've ever grown it. Almost always, 12- to 18-inch stems can be cut, and it's not unusual to cut a dozen buds and blooms at one time on one stem.

We have found that most cut roses last longer when the stem is free of a lateral joint. In order to obtain a longer stem, I have many times cut stems with one or more lateral joints, and sometimes it's worked fine; I could not tell the difference in those cut with or without this joint. However, on other occasions some of these joints apparently do not allow the rose to "drink" sufficient water because it begins to exhibit a limber neck almost immediately. When this happens, cut the stem above the joint and apply the "hot water treatment" described on page 92. If caught in time, we've never had this procedure fail to refresh the rose.

The best advice we ever had regarding stem-cutting was to learn to carefully observe the plant, cane by cane, then the bush as a whole. Canes that are left with excessive length will produce smaller roses. Conversely, when canes are cut too much,

you'll be robbing yourself of the opportunity for blooms. Trial and error, rose by rose, is the best teacher, along with some first-hand advice from an experienced grower.

One of these growers, who was not a Florida rose grower but a North Carolinian and a lifelong farmer, took the greatest pleasure from his dozen or so roses in a fenced area along his east pasture. He never bothered himself to keep up with their names. He simply loved them for the beauty they added to his life and to others. On numerous occasions as he looked at his bushes, he'd point out a cane, saying, "Now there's one I shoulda cut this spring," or "There's one I'll cut just as soon as that pretty bud blooms. I'll take it in the house to Mary... She's my wife."

In one way or another what he was saying was that if a rose bush is observed closely enough, it will, in its own way, show not only which canes to cut, but where to cut them (a philosophy that applies to roses growing not only in Florida and North Carolina but also over the rest of the country). More times than not, the cane will have at least one reddish "eye," the bud on a stem just waiting to become a lateral. This "eye" is not difficult to see; however, it emerges in different places on the canes from bush to bush. Once a cane is pruned just above this "eye," it's interesting—and telling—to note how quickly the bush responds with a new lateral cane. A bud and bloom won't be far behind.

Venus hangs low o'er the swamp
Fishes jumpin' in the pond...
Roses bloomin' in the garden
As the wren keeps callin' to his Love...
Oh, what a beautiful morning.

ROSES TO GIVE

A part of our wooden country house in the backwoods of Glades County runs over with bottles and jars, cut-off plastic containers, and other vessels that will hold enough water for cut roses. This "entry room" is really Joe Pete's domain—he's our 18-pound tomcat—but he kindly allows us to use this area between the carport and the main part of the house. It's a big room, with a high ceiling and big country cupboards that double as a pantry. The freezer is here, plus two refrigerators, one of them being the old General Electric we call the "rose 'frigerator." It's also used for fruit and vegetables when it's not full of roses.

Roses—in fact, flowers of any kind, as well as vegetables and fruits—keep better in a refrigerator that is not an automatic defrost model. Frost-free refrigerators dry out everything that's not covered or sealed. This old one looks as if it came from the nearest appliance graveyard. We don't even know how old it is because we bought it for $35 at a used appliance center twenty-some years ago and it was an antique then! Nevertheless, it's a jewel for roses, and the minute it stops working we'll be out looking for another of its kind to replace it. Another good characteristic of this old 'frigerator is that unlike our 1990s model in the kitchen, it's blessedly quiet—it doesn't vibrate when it turns off and on. It's so quiet that you have to put your ear right next to it to tell whether it's running.

In spite of the refrigerators and freezer, Joe Pete's big box, The Captain's framing materials and equipment, and Mama's old Singer sewing machine, the bottles, jars, buckets, baskets and such somehow find sittin' room, too. The jumbled assortment of containers is for the roses that we give away. Only rarely do we give cut roses that are not in water. For although I do—sometimes—cut and give them immediately, this is not the best thing for their longevity. Cut roses will last up to twice as long if they are properly cut and conditioned. We condition roses in the old 'frigerator, then place them in the containers with room-temperature tap or pond water, whichever is handier at the time, and they're ready to go.

Our emphasis is not on "arranging" roses to give away, per se; we simply place them in whatever holds water that has a pleasing appearance. There are many products that come in shapely glass bottles and jars that (after removing the labels) make very pretty, satisfactory rose containers. There is something homey and natural about placing roses in a shining clean bottle or jar to give away, saying "No need to return it." A throw-away container, as opposed to a store-bought vase—even a very inexpensive one—does not make the recipient feel compelled to return it, nor to feel guilty about keeping it, or even about throwing it away. The emphasis is entirely on the roses, not on their arrangement or on the container. After all, home-garden roses have an aura all their own. One bud, a dozen, or more—some big, some little, some perfect, some not-so-perfect—carry a special, unspoken message.

In the matter of hauling or delivering roses in a car (or truck, in our case) it helps to keep several old country crocks on hand. These squarish stoneware containers are heavy, with thick sides. Ours were passed down to us through the family; as I remember, Mother Oehlbeck said they were so old she had no idea where they originally came from. When we left North Carolina she gave us her two, one small and one large, and since then our ranch neighbor Emmie Taylor (who particularly loves any rose that's pink) gave us an old, cracked one saying, "This belonged to my mother. Now it belongs to you." Then, smiling, she quickly added, "It's for bringing pink roses to me!" Never mind the cracks—Captain glued and repaired it, and now it works fine. We simply place a bottle or jar in one of these old crocks and stuff wadded newspaper around it to prevent it from jostling around. We've found this method of transporting roses in containers to be just about foolproof. The heavy crocks are very stable, and the crumpled newspaper keeps their contents from tipping over.

Sweet dreams Sweet Prince,
Sweet dreams Little Rose...
We'll see you both come morning.

TRANSPORTING ROSES WITHOUT WATER

Naturally, it's highly desirable to transport roses in water whenever possible. However, cut roses can be successfully transported without water provided some basic rules are followed.

(1) Roses that are to be transported without water should be cut in bud only, that is, with sepals down and only the outer petals beginning to unfurl.

(2) These buds must be properly conditioned. Specifically, their stems should be cut under water as described on page 89 and place them in the refrigerator, preferably for several hours or overnight.

(3) Soak newspaper in water, then lay flat half a dozen sheets or so. Place roses one at a time on the stack of paper. Gently roll one rosebud in a single sheet, wrapping bud, stem and foliage just enough to cover it. Then place the next bud at the base of the first, wet-wrapped bud and carefully roll it the same way. Continue doing this until you have a bundle. To keep the bundle secure, use rubber bands or bands of masking tape.

(4) Place the bundle(s) flat in a heavy box, or wrap them in heavy plastic. Naturally, the vehicle you transport them in should be air-conditioned.

(5) When you arrive at your destination, unwrap the roses carefully. Cut about an inch off each stem under water, then place the roses in warm water and refrigerate them again. After the water has completely chilled, the roses will be ready to arrange.

HOT WATER TO THE RESCUE

It's not unusual for roses to quickly deplete all the water in a vase, causing them, literally, to die of thirst. More times than I like to recall, this very thing has happened, especially when slender, blown-glass bud vases are used, which are uniquely becoming to certain roses. Thus the question: Can a withered rose be revived? If the wilt has not progressed to the dehydration stage, the answer is yes, more times than not. Somewhere along the way, I read that wildflowers will respond to hot water, but not at all to cold water. With nothing to lose, I tried using the hot water treatment described below on numbers of different roses. Much to my delight, it worked! Not just once, but nearly every time—except, of course, when the rose had become dehydrated all the way to the bloom.

When a cut rose is on a relatively short stem that's growing off another cane, the resulting joint sometimes restricts the ability of the stem to conduct water to the bloom. This failure happens often enough that I try to watch the bloom for signs of distress. If it begins to wilt, I first try recutting the stem to eliminate the joint and replacing it in fresh, room temperature water. If the petals do not revive, I give the rose the hot water treatment.

A third time to use hot water is when for special reasons it seems necessary to cut roses during midday. At such times, as far as I know, the only successful way to avoid immediate and devastating wilting is to take a container of very warm (almost hot) water, and immediately upon cutting the rose, plunge the stem deep into the hot water, recutting the stem end on a slant under the surface of the water. Do not be tempted to linger in the garden! Take the roses indoors as quickly as possible and hurry to the nearest refrigerator. Let the roses stay there until the water is cool to cold. Even fifteen minutes of refrigeration will make a big difference. If a refrigerator is not available, place the roses on the floor in the coolest spot for several hours. Although this method has not failed me yet, I discourage midday cutting because the vase life of roses cut at that time will be lessened.

What to do: Cut the stem of the wilted rose to not more than 6 to 8 inches, and strip off all but two or three leaflets. Fill an 8- to 10-inch jar or vase with VERY warm water. Cut the stem on a severe slant under water, and place the rose in the jar with hot water up to its neck. It's very important for the water to be all the way up to the neck of the bloom. If the rose cannot lean against the jar top to hold it up, prop the head up with whatever will work. Immediately place the jar in the refrigerator and leave it there for several hours, until the water is thoroughly chilled.

I'm always amazed and elated at how well this works. Perhaps there are other methods of reviving wilted flowers but this is the one that works for me.

It's interesting to test the petals to determine how long this method of reviving takes. Lightly touch the petals. Chances are, in about an hour you'll be able to feel a sturdiness in the petals instead of a wilted, limp feeling. Some roses revive quickly, others can take up to several hours. The longer the stem and the larger the rose, the longer it will take.

Daybreak…
Solemn silence over the garden…
Until the red rose wakens.

HOW QUICKLY OR SLOWLY WE OPEN

Different rose varieties vary greatly in how quickly they open once they are cut. Some are like those people who, upon first awakening, bounce out of bed as if on a springboard, while others greet the day in low gear, slowly but steadily unfolding life and limb to the new day.

For instance, 'St. Patrick' opens slowly and methodically—retaining its classic form literally for days. When cut in tight bud just after the sepals have fallen it will unfailingly open slowly, day by day, until it reaches its full bloom stage of maturity some seven days later. A case in point: Our neighbors Lynn and Rusty Woods grow superb roses, but do not yet have 'St. Patrick.' So when our newly-acquired bush was in full bloom, we took them the biggest and best on the bush, knowing how they would value not only the superlative bud form and longevity, but its unique lemon color with a delicate wash of green. After exactly seven days, Lynn called, saying "Last night Rusty said to please throw out 'St. Patrick,' that he'd looked at it until he was bored!" Then she went on to say, "Of course, I didn't throw it out—but I did move it from his chair-side table."

Even when cut as a tight bud, 'Sun Flare' (a yellow Floribunda) bounces to the light of day quickly—and, I must add, always joyfully. However, its vase life is short. Even in view of its limited duration as a vase flower, a grouping of blossoms cut at different stages—some as color just begins to show between sepals not yet fallen, some

when sepals have just fallen, and others in the stage of bloom that's about half-blown, mixed free-form all together in a favorite container with stems un-wired—exhibit a lovely cheer, not unlike the bush itself when in full bloom.

Other roses that open quickly include 'Fragrant Cloud,' 'Dolly Parton,' 'Carefree Beauty,' 'Nana Mouskouri,' and 'Gypsy Dancer.' Naturally, there are countless others. These are simply a few that grow in our own garden.

As mentioned above, 'St. Patrick' is probably at the head of the list of extraordinary roses for persistence. Others that deserve longlasting accolades include 'Secret,' 'Natalie,' 'Crystaline,' 'White Knight,' 'Classic Touch,' and 'Belinda's Dream.' Three others that are at their best full-blown are 'Permanent Wave,' 'Hannah Gordon,' and 'Lady of the Dawn.' These three are considered full-face roses, rather than classic "bud" form varieties.

Of all the reds I've ever cut, nothing surpasses the longevity of 'Don Juan' as a cut rose. We've never had 'Olé' in our Florida garden, so we can't say about its performance here, but in North Carolina and Virginia it had superb lasting qualities on the bush, and in the vase it exhibited a striking similarity to a carnation. In fact, I remember a time when I was committed to produce an arrangement of red carnations for some special occasion in Charlotte, North Carolina. For some reason red carnations were extraordinarily difficult to find at that time, but there were several 'Olé' bushes in full bloom. Thinking there was nothing to lose, I cut every 'Olé' rose I could find, stripped the foliage and surrounded each bloom with various greenery and baby's breath. If anyone at the function ever noticed that the "carnation" arrangement was actually composed of 'Olé' roses, nothing was ever mentioned.

Another nontraditionally-shaped rose with grand longevity is 'Permanent Wave,' a watermelon-red Floribunda with curly, ruffled petals and very long stems that grows more like a huge Polyantha than a Floribunda.

For longest vase life, cut about a half-inch off the bottom of each stem every other day and replace roses in fresh, room-temperature water. As to whether the use of additives in the water increases vase life, I think I've tried them all and cannot honestly say that I've been able to see any difference. The commercial products that florists use do no harm and they may help. The others—7-Up®, aspirin, sugar, et cetera—seem to be of no value. I do, however, believe that it is of considerable value to rinse vases and utensils with Clorox®. It is not necessary to rinse the vase with water afterwards; any minute amount of Clorox® that is left will help sterilize the vase. Boiling water has also been recommended for the purpose, but for me, using boiling water to clean vases is inviting disaster. If a vase is stained, I often soak it with Clorox® overnight. To remove stains caused by mineral build-up from hard water, use Lime-A-Way®.

Other than the variety, significant factors affecting vase life are the freshness of the rose itself, making the cut under water, using lukewarm or room temperature water, keeping cut roses entirely away from blowing air conditioning or heat (including fans), and of course, keeping them out of sunlight.

Morning glows on my white rose
As butterflies
Poise in supplication.

5. Rose Potpourri

THE OLD STOOP

Our old plank stoop in the corner of the west porch and the dining room has seen its best days. The weather-worn boards are now cracked and discolored. Yet the idea of replacing it with a new one doesn't do much for us. After all, this old one has unique characteristics all its own.

The 20-some roses growing along its west side, three 'Don Juans' being closest in the corner, are continually decorating those old planks with their petals. Since this small collection of bushes is in full view of the dining room table—which serves more as a landing strip than a dining table—I try to use enough will power not to cut all the blooms, especially the 'Don Juans.' Thus the petal pattern on the plank floor is continually changing—making me think that Van Gogh might be testing new paints and brushes for another masterpiece. The petals catch in the cracks, which help keep them from blowing away, and with no roof, dew keeps them fresh an incredibly long time.

Not long ago I went out to check the morning from the vantage point of that stoop, of course looking at the roses rather than where I was walking, when suddenly there was a cracking sound and just as suddenly I couldn't move my left foot. My old garden boot had found the worst worn board, breaking through one end. The boot was solidly wedged in the broken board but not my foot, being protected by the boot.

After surveying the roses and watching the wild turkeys having their breakfast from cracked corn thrown out at daybreak—deciding-time had come.

None of the boards were in really good condition but only the one my boot was stuck in was actually beyond repair. Maybe the time had come to replace the whole thing and be done with it. But then, we looked at how those old boards just seemed to fit right there with a feeling of long-standing comfort blending into the whole scene as if they had grown there. I couldn't help but think of the two of us—how we have put down our roots and grown into this old place in much the same way—how we seem to fit with long-standing comfort, as if we have been growing right here in this very spot all our lives. Maybe we'll have to have a little repairing done some day in one place or another, but I don't think we could ever be transplanted.

After looking a little more and another cup of coffee, the question of whether to replace or repair sort of decided itself.

We replaced two boards and put some extra nails in a couple others which had begun to turn up on the ends.

By the time we got back in the house and looked out across the landing-strip-table to survey what we had done, or not done, a fresh new batch of petals had already fallen…

The wonder of an April wind!
Falling…floating…one by one…
See! Old stoop has a new carpet of petals.

'LADY BANKSIA' DOWN HERE AND UP YONDER

Living here in the land of flowers and sunshine, we can enjoy roses the full length of the year, but there are great joys "up yonder" that we do not have, one being the 'Lady Banksia' rose. Every spring, we long to see her flowing, full cascades of glorious, creamy-yellow roses. Her small, pompon blooms are usually about one inch in diameter. Left unpruned, 'Lady Banksia' can climb 30 to 40 feet, scaling trees or spilling over a roof, or decorating a falling-down barn.

From the San Mateo County Rose Society newsletter (Jack and Norman Bennett, editors) comes this story about this species rose that was, according to *Modern Roses 9*, first cultivated over 200 years ago in 1796.

A cutting from Scotland was sent to a gentle Scotch bride in Arizona. Mary had moved to Tombstone with her husband. She was not only lonely, but missed the wonder of the fresh green spring and the flowers of her native land. Then one memorable day, the stagecoach brought her a package, a gift of a rose slip from one of the bushes in her mother's rose garden. After the rose slip had been planted, it grew and grew until today Mary's 'Lady Banksia' has become the largest living rosebush in the world with as many as 200,000 blooms resembling a huge snow bank.

'Lady Banksia' has her own likes and dislikes, one of the former being to live in a climate that lets her "sleep and rest" during wintertime. 'Lady Banksia' is classed as a one-time-a-year performer, and that performance is, without fail, early spring. Although there may be a few scattered blooms here and there in the fall, this is the exception rather than the rule.

As to her care, she is probably as near to a no-care rose as exists. There are countless examples of 'Lady Banksia' growing in good soil and not-so-good, and rarely with fertilizer or water not provided by Mother Nature. She even grows on deserted farms through the Carolinas, particularly along U.S. Highway 1, a road that practically became a back road after the completion of I-95.

Much preferring back roads to interstates, we use "Old Number One" when we head north for family visiting. Our last trip was at peak blooming time, not only for 'Lady Banksia' but for wisteria as well. Farm after farm, on houses and barns barely standing, the rose and lacy clouds of wisteria inundated many of those falling-down structures. And many a lone pine was draped to the top with one or both. On the return home from this particular trip, petals of the blooms from both rose and wisteria had just dropped, and there beneath those enormous Carolina pines were solid carpets of mingled pale yellow and lavender petals. As we looked up and around, we could see the last few scattered petals floating downward to add another layer to the carpet. Suddenly, I thought of the day when The Captain first took me to the land of sunshine. Heading west, east of Fort Myers, near the hamlet of Alva, there was a blanket of vivid lavender-blue on the ground between a small cottage and State Road 80 with not a blade of grass showing. The entire expanse of yard was one unbroken carpet of petals beneath wide-spreading limbs of a tree growing almost in the middle. We had no idea as to the identity of the tree, so down the road a short distance, we stopped at a country store and inquired. "Oh yes," the man who was minding the store said, "You must be new here… else you'd know that's a jacaranda tree. I wisht that tree was right here in front of my store so's I could see it all day."

In *Modern Roses 9* there is this about 'Lady Banksia':

"*R. banksiae* Aiton fil. (*R. banksiana* Abel; Banks' Rose; Banksian Rose; 'Lady Banks' Rose). Sp. (Cult. 1796). Fl. wh. or yellow about one inch in diameter, on slender pedicels in many-fid. umbels; slightly fragrant; Fol. evergreen; Cl. (20 ft. or more) growth; Early spring bloom; C. and W. China; Banksianae; (14) This entry refers to more than one clone."

According to the *Handbook for Selecting Roses*, 'Lady Banksia' is eligible for Dowager Queen. Her rating is from 8.2 to 9.1. It is one of those cultivars that is most often grown on its own roots.

The pond, a silent mirror…
reflecting roses larger than life,
as is my love for them.

THE ROSE IS THE KEY
THAT UNLOCKS THE MEMORIES
by Tricia Pursley

For as long as roses have been—which is a long time considering that fossils have been discovered proving their existence for some 35 million years—there has been an insatiable fascination that goes way beyond planting and growing them. It is an enchantment difficult if not impossible to describe.

There are those who say that if one word from all the languages had to be chosen which would faithfully depict the essence of this magnetic allure, that word would have to be love.

Tricia Pursley does not dig holes and plant, nor spray or feed, nor any of the other routine earthly tasks that bring a rose into being. Yet, her romance with roses is no less powerful than if she did.

TP's joyous psalm to roses is purely a passion rarely felt, let alone expressed… a love song that could only be "sung" by one who cherishes every element, every scented petal of a rose as she does.

I carefully bend the rose petals, arching and coaxing them gently backwards upon themselves. It is hands-down, no contest, my favorite job in the flower shop which is a part of my family's business started by my father some sixty years ago. I persuade the barely open heads into becoming luminous angel-skin rose faces perfect for the bride's bouquet. I know of no other flower that will acquiesce (with enthusiasm!) to such direction. My fingers are amazed. But wait, as I sit and work, it is the flower that manipulates me: transforming the present into the past, and lingering in the air just long enough to punctuate history with indelible vignettes. The memories invoked by this fragrant muse remind me at ordinary times of the joy and sorrow of who I am.

With each petal I fold, I drift farther away from today. Cluttered with friends, family and workers assembled for the painstaking task of last minute wedding flower work, the raucous design room becomes like frost on a window pane as I wipe clear a small hole in the glass to peer into my past. Abracadabra please and thank you, I am almost a child again. The sharp staccato sound of the florist's snips become the long ago and distant clinking of glasses. I have been exiled to my bed by the big bad curfew and from my room I can hear the toasts to freedom and friendship wafting up from the lively downstairs of our old two story house, off limits to me, spy child extraordinaire. The attic fan is causing the house to breath in the night air and as my pajama-ed feet hit the floor and I tiptoe to the open window I am intoxicated by the heady fragrance. Spicy. Smokey. No. Spicysmokeysweet. Perched on the sill I peer down into our backyard garden at the adult party and discover the source of the aroma. There they are, in gossamer summer dresses: exotically beautiful ladies with roses in their hair. Burnt molasses colored aqueous eyes flutter like butterflies at half speed at the pencil-thin mustached men smoking cigars and drinking *Cuba libres*. All the while the heat from the women's heads causes flirtatious fumes to pulsate through the air. My mother is the most exquisite of all, stunning and stylish in white, sleeveless and tight; the coral rose in her hair the size of a dessert plate. Festive as it is there is a sweet sadness in the air.

Much later I would learn what my parents knew that night: that soon these dear Cuban friends, the Torrientes, the honored party guests, for whom every rose in the garden had been cut, would lose their home and their country. To this very day, I detect the faintest, fondest hint of fine Cuban cigars when I smell a rose, any rose.

On the wings of a memory-evening
Drifts the bittersweet scent of roses.

A ROSE BY ANY OTHER NAME WOULD ALWAYS SMELL
(BUT MIGHT NOT SELL)
by Dr. Derek Burch

"Look at these shrubs over here."

"No wonder they keep them at the back of the nursery! Two or three quite strong branches coming up from close to the ground, good color to the leaves but the lower parts all bare and ugly."

"And the thorns! All the way up the stems, spaced just far enough apart to allow a tentative grip, but recurved and waiting to rake your arm if it gets within striking distance."

"What about the planting and growing instructions? Let me see that nice full-care tag. What a shame the end is torn off. Okay, it says they need full sun."

"That's easy."

"Good drainage."

"What else with our soils!"

"Rich soil holding nutrients and moisture."

"Might manage that by digging in a lot of peat moss or that well-rotted compost you've been saving."

"pH slightly on the acid side of neutral."

"Not too hard in the summer place in the middle of the state, but not so easy in Miami-Dade. Perhaps a raised bed with even more peat moss."

"But this recommendation for the use of dolomite? Doesn't that make the soil less acid?"

"Maybe they are a bit confused. Do you remember seeing that article about good fertilizer practice that said that some people make a mix of ten or a dozen materials capped off with alfalfa pellets?"

"Alfalfa pellets? Eye of newt, toe of frog. Why not keep rabbits, give them the alfalfa and use the droppings for fertilizer? The rabbits would at least give you something warm and furry to come home to."

"Fertilize three weeks after planting and every three weeks after that—what sort of appetite do these plants have? Water thoroughly two or three times a week, do not wet foliage."

"Are these instructions for Florida? Perhaps they want to make a tie-in sale of little umbrellas for each bush. I wonder what colors they come in, it might be quite a conversation piece."

"What does it say about pests and diseases?"

"Spider mites, aphids, flower thrips and leaf-cutter bees—could be worse, but diseases: black-spot, mildew, crown gall—spray at least once a week during the summer covering both sides of the leaf, more often if a shower comes too soon after spray application."

"Oh, my word, there goes the neighborhood water supply."

"I wish these things had a name on them. Check one of the other tags."

"Oh, look at this, they are roses. I love roses, we always had them when I was growing up, and they smelled so good."

"Roses, yes, I love roses, too. Let's get some. We can dig up the front garden and make a nice big raised bed for them. How many do you think we've got room for? See how much they are, and while you are about it, ask the man what else we should be buying."

Oh, don't be sad... be glad!
These are not tear drops on my petals...
They're pearly dewdrops.

Growing Roses With...
JIM SCRIVNER

Jim and Mary Scrivner are the proprietors of Scrivner's Nursery & Garden Center in Fort Myers, Florida. Jim is the host of the weekly television program "Green Thumb Gardener," seen on NBC TV20 in Fort Myers.

"Over 20 years ago, Mary and I stood at the entrance of our nursery in Fort Myers watching a panel truck pulling in. We had just purchased the nursery and this was our first shipment of roses. You can probably guess who stood there with us—our friend whom we now call 'Rosebud.' She and her husband, Dr. Luther Oehlbeck, had just moved to Lee County and were in the process of planting their first Florida rose garden at their home in Alva.

"Fact is, the Oehlbecks and the Scrivners arrived in Southwest Florida about the same time.

"Rosebud and I had talked on the phone about 'Fortuniana' rootstock roses but at that time neither of us had had enough experience with the basics of that rootstock to be very knowledgeable. Nevertheless, we were convinced that it stood to reason that a Florida rootstock could produce "bigger 'n better" roses than a northern rootstock.

"Well, she didn't just stand there looking at that first truckload of roses, she helped me unload every one of them!

"And that was the beginning of Scrivners' romance with roses. At that time, there was only one place to buy from… Nelsons' Florida Roses in Apopka. As I remember, that load of budded and blooming roses sold out in a real short time and we kept ordering more and attracting more rose customers.

"Being used to bare root roses in Connecticut, it took me a good while to get used to roses growing in pots, let alone budded and blooming and ready to lift out of the container with its root ball intact. Easiest way in the world to plant a rose. I don't think many people realize what a difference there is in effort and time it takes in planting bare root roses and those grown in pots. And besides, just think of the instant results.

"From time to time we still hear that old line… 'You can't grow roses in Florida.' Well, let me tell you: that's an old wives tale that needs to be buried deep under the roses! I won't try to convince you—this book will do that—but I go on record saying that Florida is the greatest place to grow roses, and we can prove it.

"During these 20-plus years that we've been here, a couple other 'Fortuniana' rootstock growers have begun operations, so eventually, from time to time, we were able to get a better selection of varieties. Naturally, no one grower can grow every variety. We learned a long time ago that the best policy for us is to take what we can get as long as the bushes are a reasonable size and in a healthy condition.

"Probably the most significant happening in the world of Florida roses was the Jackson & Perkins' decision to begin grafting/growing selected varieties of their roses on 'Fortuniana.' Consequently, we can now offer our customers more varieties and, of course, the name Jackson & Perkins is known and honored all over the world.

"Another thing: even though I'm in the nursery business, sometimes it's hard for me to believe how many new products have come on the market to control fungus diseases such as blackspot and mildew. I'm not a preacher, but I'll say loud and long that blackspot is no longer difficult to control. It just takes a little time to spray the bushes every seven to ten days with the right ingredients. And I personally know many home garden growers who average spraying about every twelve days. Naturally, if a problem begins to surface, that's the time to spray. And depending upon the severity or extent of the problem, spray again in four to five days. As soon as the problem is gone, simply go back to the regular schedule. And, it should go without saying, that any plant which gives—produces—as much as a rose must be generously and regularly fed and watered."

"I KNOW WHO TO CALL"
by Diana Richards

My friends have come to see me… and the roses.

And they ask: What is the difference between spider mites and thrips?

Of course, I know that "thrips" rhymes with "rose hips" and spider mites are a gigantic web away from the green garden spider I cherish in the folds of fragrant blooms filling the cranberry vase.

How beautiful, the fragile bridge of silver thread between 'Carefree Beauty' and 'Queen Elizabeth.' Yes, I said. Carefree. I'm sure it was developed just for me.

And when the consuming pests that love roses as much as I do show up—and they do arrive with amazing regularity—appropriately, I do the right thing: I call Barbara and ask.

Being an artist doesn't give me artist's license for the ongoing procrastination with the precious beauty of my garden. The sun illuminates it through the morning mist, touching each blemish with tiny tears of moisture, so it flourishes in spite of my not spraying, and my over-diligence in fertilizing.

Fifty-two bushes sounds extravagant, and these friends ask, "How many?" Seeing the luscious mass of pink in the center of the table, their gaze turns toward the window that frames the garden. It's then they view for the first time my collection of skinny bushes with not-so-full foliage, and even that is pale… some not even a foot tall.

But I am always ready with the answer: I just trimmed them back.

In spite of me—my attention to them or lack of it in over-doing and under-doing—they give and keep on giving, almost as if they had not noticed.

Diana Richards lives on Hickey's Creek in Alva, Florida.

The sun
Rose full of fire
And climbed the day to noon—
Then with a sigh
Slid down the sky
Still smiling on the roses.

DR. MARGARET PFLUGE AND DR. WALTON GREGORY

They had so many loves in the garden, yet it was roses that captured their hearts, although they did not have a rosary as such. A few old English cultivars sprawled high in front of their wide, east-facing windows, and a few known for their fragrance bordered the slate walkway to the front door of their old English home at Alva, Florida.

Naturally, we became devoted friends through our mutual love of roses. As botanists, Dr. Margaret and Dr. Walton (as we affectionately called them) were overjoyed that this book was in progress. They both reviewed and critiqued page after page, and finally chapter after chapter. Neither took anything for granted. The slightest question had to be answered thoroughly, scientifically.

In the final months of the writing, Dr. Walton became gravely ill. Dr. Margaret had been invited to write a piece for the book, but caring for her husband, staying by his side day and night, left no time for writing. However, only hours after his death, she handed me a small envelope with the following note tucked inside:

June 25, 1998, 3:00 a.m.

'St. Patrick'—green tinge on yellow petals. 'Just Joey'—a brush of buff on golden yellow petals. 'Uncle Joe,' 'Legend,' and 'Don Juan' with small differences in the red colorings. 'Color Magic,' 'Double Delight,' and 'Gardens of the World' with their shadings from petal base toward petal margins. Don't forget the delicacy of 'Lady of Dawn' or the rich curves in petals of 'Permanent Wave.' And for fragrance: 'Angel Face.'

Most of all I shall always remember the look of cheer and delight when my husband rose out of his last illness at the sight of Barbara Oehlbeck with an armful of roses especially for him. The memory of that suddenly brightened face helps me now.

Then I've learned a bit about sources of rose variety names. A rose may smile by different names in different countries.

Oh, I know so little, but that little does mean a lot!

(signed) Dr. Margaret Pfluge Gregory
Alva, Florida

I went to my garden just after dawn
The roses were pearled with dew...
The first golden rays of the sun played around
Under a sky of indigo blue*.

*Dr. Walton Gregory's favorite color.

CONCLUSION

After everything's been said and the work all done, in the inimitable world of roses, it's heartening to know—to be reminded—that anyone can grow one rose or more.

The necessary ingredients are simply a bush, a pocket of earth, or a container with enough soil to accommodate roots of the bush. Sunlight is an absolute necessity as is sufficient water and food on a reasonably regular schedule. Given these basic ingredients, a rose will grow and bloom, bringing beauty and pleasure and that sense of wonder as to how one flower can exhibit such inexplicable joy and beauty.

With these minimal requirements, this is not to promise a "show rose," but it is to promise the sweet satisfaction of seeing the world's most beloved and honored flower grow and bloom as a direct result of your own efforts… even a Miniature on a narrow window sill or a balcony ledge a dozen stories high which could necessitate moving the plant twice a day—or maybe more—to give it sufficient sunlight.

And if you're wondering about the worth of all this—well, one bloom will probably provide the answer.

I give you a rose…
It is my fingers and my feet
My heart and hope,
The joy of earth and sun and rain.

I give you a rose…
It is my love for life…
It is for You.

Swan Song

When all is said and done:
Remember me as one who loved
 Roses and raindrops,
  Strawberries and springtime
  Young snow on old stumps
  Firelight and twilight...
Little ponds of water and miles of cresting waves!
  The golden glow of broom sage...
  Lichens on the fence
  Moonlight on the meadow
  Morning with the roses
And You.

APPENDIX A
GLOSSARY FOR ROSARIANS
Courtesy Richard Hedenberg and Russ Bowermaster,
ARS Consulting Rosarians, Bradenton-Sarasota Rose Society

AARS – All-America Rose Selections, an association of commercial rose growers.

ACID SOIL – Soil with a pH reaction below 7.0; a sour soil.

ADJUVANT – Substance added to a solution to aid its action.

ALKALINE SOIL – Soil with a pH reaction above 7.0; a sweet soil.

ANTHRACNOSE – A spot fungus similar to blackspot, but more common on climbing roses.

APHIDS – Plant lice. Soft-bodied sucking insects feeding on buds and new shoots.

APICAL DOMINANCE – Nature's way of producing blooms only at the top, or apical tip, of the plant and suppressing lateral bud and bloom growth below.

ARS – American Rose Society.

ATTAR OF ROSES – The pure oil extracted from rose petals.

AXIL – The angle between the upper side of a leaf and the supporting stem or cane.

BALLING – Failure of fully-developed buds to open, which may be caused by thrips or wet weather, when outer petals of blooms adhere together.

BARE ROOT – A dormant plant sold without soil around its roots.

BASAL BREAK – A new growth, starting from the bud union near the base of the plant.

BIODEGRADABLE – The ability of a material to readily decompose in the soil through the action of such microorganisms as bacteria and fungi.

BLACK FLOWER BEETLES – Daytime visitors, prefer eating pollen of light colored blooms. Not unusual to see them congregated in one bloom; seasonal.

BLACKSPOT – A fungus disease recognized by dark spots on leaves, often surrounded with bright yellow tissue, causing debilitation and eventual defoliation.

BLIND GROWTH – A lateral stem that does not terminate in a bud.

BLUING – The tendency of some varieties, especially reds, to take on a bluish shading as they fade.

BOTRYTIS BLIGHT – Fungus which appears as gray mold on buds and blooms in wet weather, often causing balling.

BRACT – Undeveloped leaf, normally just below the flower head.

BROADCAST – Scattering fertilizer and other nutrients evenly over a soil surface.

BROWN GARDEN BEETLES – Arrive at night and feed in blooms.

BUD – An immature, undeveloped flower at the top of a stem or in a leaf axil.

BUD EYE – A vegetative node found where a leaf joins a stem at a leaf axil; also called a scion.

BUD UNION – The joint where a scion, the upperstock, is joined with the understock.

BUDDING – Method of propagating by taking a bud from a stem at a leaf axil and inserting it under the bark of an understock.

BUD WOOD – A portion of a cane containing several bud eyes or scions at each leaf axil.

BUDWORMS – Small caterpillars feeding in or on opening buds.

BUFFERING AGENT – Substance added to a solution that alters the acidity or alkalinity.

CALCINATED CLAY – Kitty litter; highly absorbent natural material with nutrient-holding capacity, used in rose-hole formulation.

CALCIUM (Ca) – Nutrient that holds cell walls together and promotes stability and early growth.

CAMBIUM LAYER – The layer of cells between the bark and stem of the plant, only one cell thick.

CANDELABRA – A strong, dominant cane with accelerated growth originating from the bud union, exploding into a multitude of smaller canes above the main break.

CANE – Primary growth arising from the bud union of the plant which subsequently puts forth laterals.

CANE BORERS – Bee- or wasp-like insects that tunnel into cut tips of rose canes to build nests and lay eggs.

CANKER – A localized lesion or diseased area on a woody cane.

CATERPILLARS – Wormlike larvae; many varieties are pests on roses, especially the corn earworms that feed on rose buds and blooms.

CHELATE – A chemical compound incorporating a trace element. The compound surrounds the trace element to protect it from becoming locked in the soil and makes it immediately available to the plant.

CHLOROPHYLL – The green coloring matter of leaves.

CHLOROSIS – The yellowing or loss of green color in leaves, caused by chlorophyll deficiency.

CLASSIC SHRUB – Shrub roses with a family name, such as 'Hybrid Blanda,' 'Hybrid Hugonis,' 'Kordesii.' For complete listing, see the classifications in the ARS *Handbook for Selecting Roses*.

CLIMBER – Rose variety that has long canes and can clamber up convenient structures or other plants, aided by their curved prickles.

COMPACTED SOIL – Soil packed tightly together, most often as the result of walking and trampling on beds. Reduces water and air percolation, resulting in poor growth.

COMPOST – Nutrient-rich product of decomposed raw organic matter which can be used as a fertilizer or soil additive.

CONTROLLED RELEASE – A term applied to fertilizers that release their nutrients in regulated amounts.

COROLLA – Whorl of petals growing from the receptacle of the flower (bloom).

COURT OF HONOR – A rose show court of winners consisting of (in order) Queen, King, Princess, and may include additional awards at the discretion of the local society.

CR – Consulting Rosarian. A program of the American Rose Society that appoints individuals who have demonstrated significant knowledge of rose culture and are willing to share that knowledge.

CROSSING – The act of cross pollinating one variety with another.

CROWN GALL – Bacterial disease characterized by rounded, rough-surfaced tumors on or near the bud union.

CULTIVAR – Cultivated variety; synonym for rose variety.

CUTTING – A section of stem used for propagation.

DEADHEADING – Removing dead or spent blooms to encourage reblooming.

DECORATIVE ROSE – Bloom form that tends to be loose and informal and lacking a high-pointed center. Also called garden rose.

DEFOLIATION – Loss of leaves from natural, pathological, chemical or other causes.

DIATOMACEOUS EARTH (D.E.) – Earthy deposit containing diatoms (the silica-containing bodies of microscopic algae) used in a finely pulverized state as an absorbent or filter.

DIEBACK – A disease causing canes and laterals to die back from their tips downward.

DISBUD – Removal of secondary buds to improve the size and quality of remaining bloom(s).

DOG LEG – A cane growing outward, then upward, like a dog's leg.

DOLOMITE LIME – Finely-ground dolomite limestone which will increase pH level and also supply some magnesium.

DORMANT – Cyclical period when a plant rests and its growth processes slow down, as days grow shorter and temperatures begin to drop.

DOUBLE – Rose bloom with 25 or more petals.

DOWNY MILDEW – A fungus disease causing irregular purple spots on young leaves and stems during cool, moist conditions – can be fatal to the bush.

DRIP LINE – An imaginary line around a bush directly under the outermost laterals; the point at which rain water drains off.

DRY WRAPPING – A procedure of wrapping roses in plastic wrap for holding in a state of suspended development to be revived for use days or weeks later.

ENGLISH ROSES – An informal name that describes shrub roses that are the result of crossing Old Garden Roses with modern roses.

EPSOM SALTS – Magnesium sulfate; a quick source of magnesium.

EXHIBITION ROSE – Rose bloom with a high-pointed center, with outer petals symmetrically arranged in an attractive circular outline.

EXHIBITOR – A rose hobbiest who enters home-grown roses in a show to be judged for recognition by ARS standards.

FAULT – A defect or imperfection in a rose specimen.

FERTILIZER BANDING – Placing fertilizer in soil in narrow bands, covering with soil, but not mixing.

FLORET – An individual bloom in a spray.

FLORIBUNDA – Rose class that produces smaller flowers in clusters, especially attractive for landscaping.

FLORIFEROUS – Free-flowering.

FLOWER HEAD – Collection of florets or buds that form an inflorescence.

FLUSH – A bush in full bloom all at once.

FOLIAR-FEEDING – Applying liquid fertilizer directly to plant leaves, generally in a fine spray.

FULLY-OPEN – A mature, open bloom, showing stamens.

FUNGI – Organisms that cause mildews, mold, rust, and smuts that infect plants. Those primarily affecting roses are blackspot, powdery mildew, downy mildew, and rust. *Singular* fungus.

FUNGICIDE – An agent of natural or chemical origin that controls or destroys fungi.

GARDEN ROSE – *See* Decorative rose.

GRAFTING – Form of propagation whereby a desired variety of a rose plant (the scion) is induced to unite and grow on a strong, vigorous rootstock.

GRANDIFLORA – Rose class similar to the Hybrid Tea but capable of producing blooms in clusters or sprays; a rose class resulting from crossing a Hybrid Tea with a Floribunda.

GRANULAR FERTILIZER – Plant nutrient containing nitrogen (N), phosphorous (P), and potassium (K), often including minor elements, combined with inert material in a granular form for easy broadcasting.

GREEN MANURE – A crop incorporated into the soil for the purpose of soil improvement.

GROOMING – Physical improvement of a specimen by an exhibitor before a rose show.

GROUND COVERS – An informal name for shrub roses that are low growing and spreading in habit. Generally considered low maintenance.

GUARD PETALS – Outermost petals of the bloom, often with green streaks. They protect the inner blooms while the flower is opening.

GYPSUM – Calcium sulfate, a natural material that is a beneficial soil additive.

HARDENING OFF – Standing roses in water in a cool, dark place for a period of time to allow water uptake and turgidity before refrigerating.

HARDY – Resistant to low temperatures.

HERBICIDE – Chemical used to destroy undesirable plants or weeds.

HIP – A rose fruit or seed pod.

HONEYDEW – Plant sap sucked out and then secreted by aphids, rich in sugars, attracting ants and forming a medium for growth of a black fungus known as sooty mold.

HUMUS – Spongy organic matter with a gelatinous substance binding together inorganic particles forming the soil texture.

HYBRID – Results of cross-pollination between two different varieties or species of plants.

HYBRID TEA – Roses produced after many years of crossing other roses. They produce stately blooms on long stems. The first Hybrid Tea was 'La France,' produced in 1867.

INERT MATERIAL – Material that is mixed with pesticides or fertilizers in a compound for ease of application.

INFLORESCENCE – The general arrangement and disposition of flowers on a single stem which may consist of one or more sprays.

INORGANIC MATTER – Material of mineral origin.

INSECTICIDE – Substance of natural or chemical origin used to control insects.

IPM – Integrated Pest Management, a program to promote the use of biological and other environmentally-friendly controls of insects and disease.

LADYBUG – Common name for the ladybird beetle, a ferocious consumer of aphids.

LATERAL – A secondary shoot or stem arising from a cane; smaller canes that grow from laterals are called sub-laterals.

LAYERING – Propagating technique in which the stem is bent down and buried in rooting medium to force the development of roots along the buried portion of the stem.

LEACHING – Process of removing excess soluble salts from topsoil by pouring water through the soil.

LEAF ROSETTE – A leaf cluster or tufts with no stem or bud.

LEAF SET – The number of leaflets that make up a leaf, usually five in roses, but may be from three to nine.

LEAFCUTTER BEE – A small bee that cuts ovals and circles from leaf margins for nest building; there is no known control but the bee may be beneficial as a pollinator.

LEAFHOPPER – Sucking insect on underside of leaves, producing stippled white pattern on upper leaf surface.

LEAFLET – One part of a leaf set that makes up a leaf.

LIME – A soil additive used to sweeten the soil; ground limestone, used to reduce acidity in soil, is also a supply of calcium; dolomite lime will supply some magnesium.

LOAM SOIL – Soil composed of sand, silt and clay in approximately equal parts.

MAGNESIUM (Mg) – Nutrient that promotes chlorophyll formation, which interacts to produce greener foliage.

MAJOR OR MACRO ELEMENTS – Nitrogen (N), phosphorous (P) and potassium (K).

MICROCLIMATE – Climate of a small area or locality near ground level, such as a backyard or portion of it.

MICRO ELEMENTS – Iron (Fe), manganese (Mn), boron (B), zinc (Zn), copper (Cu), molybdenum (Mo), and chlorine (Cl), usually in sufficient supply in well prepared and fertilized soil.

MINIATURE ROSE – A rose that has all the aspects of other roses but with small (miniature) foliage and blooms.

MIST PROPAGATION – A procedure using vaporized water within an enclosed space to provide constant moisture for plant rooting and grafting.

MITICIDE – Substance of natural or chemical origin used to control mites.

MODERN SHRUBS – A class of roses that does not have a family connection but is designated as a shrub (S) in the ARS *Handbook for Selecting Roses.*

MULCH – Material that covers the soil to prevent water evaporation, keep the ground cool and prevent weed growth.

NEMATODES – Microscopic worms that feed on roots in the soil, stunting plant vigor and growth.

NITROGEN (N) – Nutrient that stimulates growth of tall, strong canes, good blooms and rich, dark foliage.

NITROGEN FIXATION – The conversion of atmospheric nitrogen into complex compounds that can eventually be used by the plant.

NODE – Bulge on canes at a leaf axil where growth begins, also called a bud eye.

NPK analysis – The ratio of nitrogen (N), phosphorous (P), and potassium (K) in a plant fertilizer.

OLD GARDEN ROSES – Rose varieties that were in existence prior to 1867, when the first Hybrid Tea was produced.

ONE-BLOOM-PER-STEM – A rose bloom with no side buds.

ORGANIC MATTER – Material of plant or animal origin.

OWN-ROOT – Plant produced from cutting or seed, as opposed to being grafted or budded.

PACKAGED ROSES – Bare root roses packaged in waterproof paper with moisture-holding material around the roots.

PEAT MOSS – A long lasting, slowly decaying, organic material of greatest value as a soil additive, promoting moisture retention and improving soil structure.

PERLITE – A volcanic mineral that has been expanded by heat treatment to form lightweight, white granules used for soil conditioning and as a substitute for sand.

PEDUNCLE – The portion of stem between bloom and the first leaf set.

PEGGING – Practice of securing ends of flexible canes to the ground to induce lateral growth and blooms along the pegged cane.

PESTICIDES – Materials such as insecticides, fungicides, herbicides, and miticides used to control pests.

PETALOIDS – Small, irregular petals in center of blooms, often covering the stamens.

PHOSPHOROUS (P) – Nutrient that stimulates root growth and big blooms.

PHOTOSYNTHESIS – The forming of plant matter from carbon dioxide, water and inorganic salts, using sunlight as a source of energy with the aid of chlorophyll.

PISTIL – Female reproductive organ of the flower.

PLANT LICE – Aphids.

POLYANTHA – Rose class with clusters of small blooms that are produced almost continuously throughout the season.

PORE SPACE – The space between soil particles, where air and water percolate.

POTASSIUM (K) – Nutrient that promotes root growth and bloom color; also called potash.

POWDERY MILDEW – A fungus disease producing a white, cottony coating on plants; it later turns the leaves black and wrinkled, and is most prevalent during periods of warm days and cool nights.

PRICKLES – The correct term for rose "thorns."

pH – Symbol for the degree of acidity or alkalinity of a solution, based on a scale of 0 to 14, with 7 being neutral. Roses grow best in soil with a pH of 6.0 to 6.8.

PROPAGATION – Reproduction of plants, either from seeds (sexual reproduction) or from cuttings, budding or layering (asexual reproduction).

PRUNING – The wise removal of plant parts to obtain a more desirable and productive bush.

RAISED BEDS – Rose beds built above ground level, usually using landscape logs or railroad ties to improve and maintain good drainage, and a hedge against the tendency of new plantings to sink.

RAMBLER – Rose with long, arching canes that is not compact enough to rank as a shrub nor rigid enough to be classed as a Climber.

RECURRENT – Repeated blooming during the year.

REGISTERED ROSE – A rose that has been registered with the American Rose Society, as agent for International Registration Authority for Roses.

REMONTANT – *See* Recurrent.

ROOT BOUND – Term describing a plant with a root system too large for its container.

ROOTSTOCK – Rose variety with a vigorous root system that will accept grafting from other varieties; also called understock. The preferred rootstock for Florida is 'Fortuniana.'

ROOT ZONE – The soil area inhabited by the roots of the rose bush.

ROSE MIDGE – Small ($1/_{20}$ inch) insect that attacks the apical end of the rose, resulting in loss of bloom. Unknown in Florida.

ROSE SHOW SCHEDULE – A show program setting rules, entry classes, show chairpersons, dates and times.

SCALE – Sucking insect staying in place for life; more common on roses not pruned annually, such as Climbers.

SCION – The bud of a rose variety that is grafted onto an understock; also called the bud eye.

SEMI-DOUBLE – Rose blooms with 13 to 24 petals.

SEPALS – Modified leaves that cover the bud before it opens.

SHOVEL PRUNE – To dig out and remove an unwanted bush.

SILT – Fine, smooth, floury earth particles, smaller than sand particles, found as floating sediment in rivers and lake waters.

SINGLE – A five- to twelve-petalled rose.

SIPHON MIXER – A hose attachment device for mixing water from a spigot with a concentrated fertilizer solution at a specific rate.

SLOW RELEASE FERTILIZER – Fertilizer that provides a balance of nutrients throughout the growing season, whose action is based on moisture and/or temperature.

SOIL ADDITIVE – Any material added to the soil in order to enhance soil activity.

SOIL pH – A measure of hydrogen ion activity in the soil that expresses the degree of acidity (sourness) or alkalinity (sweetness). *See* pH.

Spading fork – A four-tined fork the size of a garden spade, used to loosen and aerate compacted soil in rose beds

SPECIES ROSE – A wild rose unchanged from its natural form that will breed true from seed.

SPECIMEN – Any stem terminating in one or more blooms.

SPIDER MITES – Tiny, spider-like creatures that thrive in hot, dry weather and attack plant leaves by sucking their juices, which may defoliate the plant.

SPLIT CENTER – Petal formation in center of bloom, forming a cleavage.

SPORT – In botany, a sudden bud variation, the offspring differing from its parent in well-marked characteristics; a lateral from a central cane bearing blooms that differ significantly from the parent; a genetic mutation.

SPRAY – A group of florets on one main or lateral stem.

SPRAY PROGRAM – A program of regular application of pesticides and/or fungicides to roses.

SPREADER-STICKER – Material added to a pesticide or fertilizer solution which causes it to spread more evenly and remain on the surface where applied.

SPURS – Short growth, only a few inches long, that has hardened off and tapered down to a point that will not produce a bloom.

STAMEN – Male, pollen-producing, reproductive organ of a flower.

STANDARD ROSE – *See* Tree rose.

STEM – Plant part that supports leaves and bloom.

STEM-ON-STEM – A primary stem and bloom with a portion of the previous stem growth still attached.

STRESS – External factors that inhibit perfect plant growth, such as heat and lack of water.

SUCKER – A shoot from a rootstock growing from below the bud union.

SULFUR (S) – A raw material for amino acids and proteins that is needed for plant health.

SYSTEMIC – A pesticide that is absorbed into the system of a plant.

THRIPS – Speck-sized, sucking insects that hide inside unopened blooms and attack buds and blooms, causing brown flecking on petal and bloom edges.

THUMB PRUNING – To rub off unwanted bud nodes after pruning; also called finger pruning.

TOP-DRESSING – Application of fertilizer, compost, or mulch material to the surface without mixing it into the soil.

TOUCH-UP PRUNING – Removal of canes or laterals that have not sprouted or grown properly.

TRANSPIRATION – Process by which moisture is emitted from plant leaves, through transmission of water absorbed through its roots.

TREE ROSE – Consists of an understock, a stem or trunk, and a head. The head can be any desired variety or classification of rose; also called a standard rose.

TURGID – Term describing plant cells having adequate moisture to cause the cells to fully expand.

UNDERSTOCK – *See* Rootstock.

VERMICULITE – A natural mica mineral that is highly water absorbent, excellent for rooting cuttings.

WATER – Single most important requirement for roses. Without water the plant cannot absorb nutrients from the soil.

WATERLOGGING – Extremely poor soil drainage that causes roots to remain wet and oxygen to the plant to be cut off, often resulting in leaves yellowing and dropping off.

WATER SOLUBLE FERTILIZER – Fertilizer soluble in water, allowing it to be immediately available to the plant when applied.

WINTERIZING – Protecting roses by various means against severe winter elements.

We do not aspire to perfection…
Only to please those who tend and love us.

APPENDIX B
ROSES THAT CAN BE GROWN IN CENTRAL FLORIDA WITHOUT SPRAYING

This list was compiled by Dr. Malcolm Manners and is reprinted here with his kind permission.

NAME	COLOR	CLASS	REPEATS?	ROOT SYSTEM	NOTES
'Agrippina'	medium red	China	constant	own-root or grafted	
'Basye's Purple Rose'	purple	Rugosa	in cycles	grafted on 'Fortuniana'	
'Belfield'	dark red	China	constant	own-root or grafted	small bush
'Belinda's Dream'	medium pink	Shrub	constant	grafted on 'Fortuniana'	good cut flower
'Bon Silene'	deep pink	Tea	constant	grafted on 'Fortuniana'	
'Carefree Beauty'	medium pink	Shrub	constant	grafted on 'Fortuniana'	
'Countesse du Cayla'	pink/orange	China	constant	own-root or grafted	
'Don Juan'	dark red	Climber	constant	grafted on 'Fortuniana'	pillar-type
'Dortmund'	bright red	Climber	in cycles	grafted on 'Fortuniana'	
'Ducher'	white	China	constant	own-root or grafted	
'Duchesse de Brabant'	pale pink	Tea	constant	grafted on 'Fortuniana'	
'Etoile de Lyon'	pale yellow	Tea	constant	grafted on 'Fortuniana'	
'Fortuniana'	white	Misc.	no	own-root	med. climber
'La Marne'	medium pink	Polyantha	constant	own-root or grafted	
'Louis Philippe'	medium red	Chins	constant	own-root or grafted	
'Maggie'	purplish red	Bourbon	constant	grafted on 'Fortuniana'	
'Marnan Cochet'	pink Blend	Tea	constant	grafted on 'Fortuniana'	
'Marechal Niel'	light yellow	Noisette	constant	grafted on 'Fortuniana'	huge climber
'Marie Van Houtte'	white/pink	Tea	constant	grafted on 'Fortuniana'	
'Mermaid'	light yellow	Climber	in cycles	grafted on 'Fortuniana'	huge climber
'Mme. Lombard'	medium pink	Tea	constant	grafted on 'Fortuniana'	
'Mons. Tillier'	red/pink/Brick	Tea	constant	grafted 'Fortuniana'	
'Mrs. B. R. Cant'	red & pink	Tea	constant	own-root or grafted	
'Mutabilis'	yellow/pink/red	China	constant	own-root or grafted	
'Old Blush'	light & dark pink	China	constant	own-root or grafted	
'Papa Gontier'	medium red	Tea	constant	grafted on 'Fortuniana'	
'Perle d'Or'	apricot	Polyantha	constant	grafted on 'Fortuniana'	
'Pink Pet'	medium pink	China	constant	own-root or grafted	
R. banksiae	white or yellow	species	no	grafted on 'Fortuniana'	big climber
R. laevigata	white	species	no	own-root or grafted	big climber
R. roxburghii	deep pink	species	in cycles	grafted on 'Fortuniana'	huge bush
'Sea Foam'	white	Shrub/Cl.	in cycles	grafted on 'Fortuniana'	moderate climber
'Souv. de la Malmaison'	light pink	Bourbon	constant	grafted on 'Fortuniana'	
'Souv. de St. Anne's'	light pink	Bourbon	constant	grafted on 'Fortuniana'	
'Spray Cécile Brünner'	pale pink	Polyantha	constant	own-root or grafted	huge bush
'St. Davids'	dark red	China	constant	own-root or grafted	
'Sun Flare'	bright yellow	Floribunda	constant	grafted on 'Fortuniana'	
'Sunsprite'	bright yellow	Floribunda	constant	grafted on 'Fortuniana'	
'Tausendschön'	pink to white	Hybrid Multiflora	spring/summer	own-root/grafted	med. climber

Most other Chinas and Rugosas, and many other Teas could also be added to this list. We have had very poor success with Rugosas unless they are grafted to 'Fortuniana' roots. Most of these varieties will show some blackspot and/or powdery mildew when the weather is ideal for those diseases. If you intend to exhibit in rose shows, some spraying may be necessary. But if you're willing to live with a few blemished leaves, all of the varieties listed will thrive and flower heavily without spraying.

APPENDIX C
THE RAMBLING ROSARIAN'S SPRAY FORMULATIONS

BLACKSPOT AND POWDERY MILDEW:

Funginex® .1 tablespoon per gallon (Triforine 6.5%)
Triforine . . . . .1 teaspoon per gallon (Triforine 18%)
Immunox (Systhane formulation) . . .2 tablespoons per gallon
Rose Defense . . . . .2 tablespoons per gallon (Neem extract)
Banner Maxx (14.3%) . . . .$^{1}/_{3}$ teaspoon per gallon (14–21 days)
Compass (50 WP) . . . .$^{1}/_{8}$ teaspoon per gallon (14 days)

DOWNY MILDEW:

Pace . . . . .1 tablespoon per gallon
Ridomil Bravo . . . . .1 tablespoon per gallon

BLACKSPOT:

Manzate 200DF (75%) . . . . .1 tablespoon per gallon
Daconil 2787® WDG (90%) . . . . . .1 teaspoon per gallon (downy mildew also)
Fungi-Gard (Daconil 11%) . . . . . . .2 tablespoons per gallon
Maneb Flowable . . . . .1 tablespoon per gallon
Cleary's 3336 . . . .$^{1}/_{2}$ teaspoon per gallon (Benomyl substitute)

SEVERE POWDERY MILDEW:

Rubigan . . . .$^{1}/_{4}$ teaspoon per gallon. Systemic, 14 days.
Systhane (Nova 40 WP) . . . .$^{1}/_{4}$ teaspoon per gallon, 14 days
Immunox® (Systhane formulation) . .1 tablespoon per gallon

CHEWING, SUCKING INSECTS:

Orthene® (9.4% EC) . . . . .2 tablespoons per gallon; thrips
Orthene® (75% SP) . . . . .2 teaspoons per gallon; thrips
Cygon 2E .2 teaspoons per gallon; thrips, whitefly
Malathion (50% EC) . . . . .2 teaspoons per gallon; effective for aphids
Insecticidal Soap (Safer®) . . . . .5 tablespoons per gallon; spot aphid control
Margosan-0 (botanical insecticide) . . .1 tablespoon per gallon

COMBINATION SPRAY—FUNGUS DISEASE AND INSECTS:

Orthenex .2 tablespoons per gallon; useful in small gardens

BEETLES, CORN EAR WORMS:

Mavrik Aquaflow . . . . .2 teaspoons per 5 gallons; broad spectrum
10% Sevin® Dust . . . . .Dust bud and bloom areas ONLY; dry foliage.

SPIDER MITES:

Water . . . . .Use water wand under leaves during hot, dry weather.
Avid . . . .$^{1}/_{4}$ teaspoon per gallon; translaminar, systemic
Stirrup M (pheromone) . . . .$^{1}/_{8}$ teaspoon per gallon; add to Avid.
Vendex . . . .$1^{1}/_{2}$ teaspoons per gallon; 21–28 day intervals

WEED CONTROL:

Roundup® . . . . .2 tablespoons per gallon; apply during active growth.

Note: Always read and follow label instructions. Products may not be registered in all states. Check with your county's Cooperative Extension Service for current information on pesticide use. The National Pesticide Telecommunications Network has a 24-hour, toll-free number to answer questions on the proper use or effects of pesticides—keep this number handy: 1-800-858-7378.

American Rose Society
8877 Jefferson Paige Road
Shreveport, LA 71119-8817
(318)938-5402

Ace Garden Center
350 West Hickpoochee/
    State Road 80 West
LaBelle, FL 33935
(863)675-2672

Boynton Botanicals
9281 87th Place South
Boynton Beach, FL 33437
(561)737-1490

Bridges Roses
2734 Toney Road
Lawndale, NC 28090
(704)538-9412
BriRoses@shelby.net
www.bridgesroses.com

Cape Nursery
1200 SW 20th Avenue
Cape Coral, FL 33991
(941)283-0598

Crowder Bros. Ace Hardware
5409 Manatee Avenue West
Bradenton, FL 34209
(941)795-8442

Dolin's Nursery
801 62nd Avenue North
St. Petersburg, FL 33702
(727)525-3434

The PlantSmith
dba Duel Ernest Roses
1555 Folsom Road
Loxahatchee, FL 33470
(561)753-9649

Galloway Farms
7790 SW 87th Avenue
Miami, FL 33173
(305)274-7472
info@gallowayfarm.com

Giles Nursery
2611 Holly Hills Cutoff Road
Davenport, FL 33837
(863)422-8103
flrose@digital.net

Green Garden Nursery
1100 North Lake Blvd.
Lake Park, FL 33403
(561)845-2072

Kerby's Nursery
2311 South Parsons Avenue
Seffner, FL 33584
(813)685-3265

Kraft Nursery
750 South Powerline Road
Deerfield Beach, FL 33442
(954)421-6960

Mills Magic Rose Mix
P O Box 2878
Cleveland, TN 37320
1-800-845-2325
www.millsmix.com

Muncy's Rose Emporium Nursery
11207 Celestine Pass
Sarasota, FL 34246
(941)377-6156
MuncyRos@gte.net

Nelsons' Florida Roses
2300 Sheeler Road
Apopka, FL 32703
800-887-1849
info@nelsonsfloridaroses.com

Orban's Nursery
9601 Ninth Avenue North
Bradenton, FL 34209
800-898-4010

Peacock Nursery
104 South Ivy
Florahoma, FL 32140
(904)659-2142

Plant Ranch Nursery
14108 Beach Boulevard
Jacksonville, FL 32250
(904)223-4546

Queen Palm Nursery
5275 North Washington Blvd.
Sarasota, FL 34234
(941)355-4004

Roseglen Gardens Heirloom Roses
11581 Riggs Road
Naples, FL 34114
(941)775-4489
RoseglenGardens@aol.com

Scrivner's Garden Center
1211 Seaboard Street
Fort Myers, FL 33916
(941)334-7006

Sunshine Growers' Supply, Inc.
4760 Taylor Road (I-75 Exit 28)
Punta Gorda, FL 33950-4719
(941)637-9999
www.sunshinegrowers.com
sunshine@cyberstreet.com

Tallahassee Nurseries
2911 Thomasville Road
Tallahassee, FL 32312
(850)385-2162
www.tallahasseenurseries.com

Wayne Hibbs Farm &
    Garden Supply
1492 4th Street
Sarasota, FL 34236
(941)366-4954

Wayside Gardens Co.
1 Garden Lane
Hodges, SC 29695-0001
1-800-845-1124
www.waysidegardens.com

FOR FURTHER READING

Allen, R. C. 1948. *Roses for Every Garden.* New York: M. Barrows.

American Rose Society. 1999. *American Rose Annual 1999.* Shreveport, LA: American Rose Society.

American Rose Society. 2001. *Handbook for Selecting Roses and ARS Exhibition Names.* Shreveport, LA: American Rose Society.

American Rose Society. 2000. *Modern Roses XI.* Shreveport, LA: American Rose Society.

American Rose Society. 2000. *Ultimate Rose.* London: Dorling-Kindersley.

Bassity, Matthew A. R. 1966. *The Magic World of Roses.* New York: Hearthside Press.

Beales, Peter. 1997. *Classic Roses.* New York: Henry Holt & Co.

Bonaparte, Josephine, and Pierre-Joseph Redoute. 1983. *Roses for an Empress.* Great Britain: Sidgwick & Jackson.

Christopher, Thomas. 1989. *In Search of Lost Roses.* New York: Summit Books.

Chotzinoff, Robin. 1996. *People with Dirty Hands: The Passion for Gardening.* New York: Macmillan.

Coats, Peter. 1962. *Roses.* London: Octopus Books.

Crockett, James Underwood, and the Editors of Time-Life Books. 1971. *Roses: The Time-Life Encyclopedia of Gardening.* New York: Time-Life Books.

Edland, H. 1962. *Roses in Color.* New York: Viking Press.

Gamble, James Alexander, 1950. *Roses Unlimited.* Harrisburg, PA: Dr. James A. Gamble.

Garden Way Publishing. 1989. *Roses: 1001 Gardening Questions Answered.* Pawnal, VT: Storey Communications, Inc.

Gordon, Jean. 1959. *Immortal Roses: One Hundred Rose Stories and Vignettes of Famous People and Events.* Woodstock, VT: Red Rose Publications.

Hessayon, Dr. D. G. 1995. *The Rose Expert.* England: Britannica House.

Hessayon, Dr. D. G., and Harry Wheatcroft. 1965. *Be Your Own Rose Expert.* UK: Pan Britannica Industries, Ltd.

Jekyll, Gertrude, and Edward Mawley. 1983. *Roses.* New Hampshire: The Ayer Company. (Originally published in 1902 as *Roses for English Gardens.*)

Kiaer, Eigil, and Verner Hancke. 1966. *The Concise Handbook of Roses.* New York: E. P. Dutton & Co.

LeGrice, E. B. 1965. *Rose Growing Complete.* UK: Faber & Faber.

MacFarland, J. Horace, and Robert Pyle. 1937. *How to Grow Roses.* New York: MacMillan.

McCann, Sean. 1991. *Miniature Roses: Care and Cultivation.* Harrisburg, PA: Stackpole Books.

McCann, Sean. 1993. *The Rose: An Encyclopedia of North American Roses, Rosarians, and Rose Lore.* Mechanicsburg, PA: Stackpole Books.

Nicolas, J. H. 1937. *A Rose Odyssey: Reminiscences of Many Trips to European Rose Centers.* New York: Doubleday, Doran & Co.

McDonald, Elvin. 1998. *Climbing Roses.* New York: Smithmark Publishers.

McDonald, Elvin. 1998. *Old-Fashioned Roses.* New York: Smithmark Publishers.

McDonald, Elvin. 1998. *Shrub Roses.* New York: Smithmark Publishers.

McDonald, Elvin. 1998. *Tea Roses.* New York: Smithmark Publishers.

McGredy, Sam, and Sean Jennett. 1972. *A Family of Roses.* USA: Dodd, Mead & Co.

McIntyre, James. 1970. *The Story of the Rose.* London: Ward Lock, Ltd.

Olds, Margaret (editor). 1999. *Botanica's Roses: The Encyclopedia of Roses for Australian Gardens.* New South Wales, Australia: Welcome Rain Publishing.

Rockwell, F. F., and Esther C. Grayson. 1966. *Rockwell's Complete Book of Roses.* New York: Doubleday & Co.

Rohde, Eleanour Sinclair. 1939. *Rose Recipes.* London: Chiswick Press, Ltd.

Scanniello, Stephen, and Tanya Bayard. 1990. *Roses of America.* New York: Henry Holt & Co.

Schneider, Peter. 1995. *Peter Schneider on Roses.* New York: MacMillan.

Seymour, Jacqueline. 1978. *Roses: The Color Nature Library.* New York: Crescent Books.

Suares, Jean-Claude, and Laura Cerwinske. 1996. *A Passion for Roses.* Kansas City: Andrews & McMeel.

Sunset Books and Sunset Magazine. 1982. *How to Grow Roses.* Menlo Park, CA: Lane Publishing Co.

Svoboda, P. 1966. *Beatuiful Roses.* London: Spring Books.

Taylor, Norman. 1986. *Taylor's Guide to Roses.* Boston: Houghton Mifflin.

Thomson, Richard. 1959. *Old Roses for Modern Gardens.* New York: D. Van Nostrand.

Warner, A. J. "Pop." 1994. *A Year in the Rose Garden: The Wit and Wisdom of Pop Warner.* Shreveport, LA: American Rose Society.

Welch, William C. 1990. *Antique Roses for the South.* Dallas: Taylor Publishing Company.

Westcott, Cynthia. 1965. *Anyone Can Grow Roses.* Fourth Edition. New York: D. Van Nostrand Co., Inc.

May the sun shine on your path every day
With roses beside you all the way.

ABOUT THE AUTHOR

A Southerner born in Hickory, North Carolina, Barbara Oehlbeck has grown roses nearly all her life, first under the tutelage of her mother in Martinsville, Virginia, where she also became an ardent naturalist. As a young woman she moved to Charlotte and entered the fields of broadcasting and journalism, producing a small volume of poetry and a biography of Bishop Herbert Spaugh. She was named to the Literary Heritage of Charlotte-Mecklenberg-North Carolina.

Nearly a quarter-century ago, Barbara and her husband, physician-photographer Dr. Luther Oehlbeck, made their first Florida home aboard their small cruiser *Sweet Thing* (thus he became "The Captain"). He has illustrated Barbara's books and diverse writings in regional, state and national publications, reflecting their combined devotion to nature, Florida images, and people who play significant roles in these areas. In 1997, Barbara's in-depth study of Florida's state tree led to the publication of *The Sabal Palm, A Native Monarch*—and to a more extensive study of native Florida flora. She was named Outstanding Horticulture Writer/State of Florida (1993–94) by the Florida Nurserymen and Growers Association, and was honored as a Florida Woman of Achievement in the Arts (2000) by Palm Beach Community College. The Oehlbecks' latest book, *Barefoot to Boots* (1997) was written with the late Charles W. Flint. Barbara's biographical manuscript—cameos of her mother's life—titled *Mama... Root, Hog, or Die* is now being serialized in the *Peace River Farmer & Rancher* newsmagazine.

The Oehlbecks live, work and grow roses in Muse, a remote, rural area of Florida's Glades County, about which she says, "In these more or less six miles squared there 'usta' be a school, a weathered general store and post office and a few little village enterprises... all gone now. However, since 1983, there's Mac's Country Store, with a coin telephone and two fuel pumps. To those of us who hope to live out our lives here, Muse is mostly a state of mind—maybe more of a myth than anything else."

The sweetest flower that grows,
I give you as we part.
For you it is a rose
For me it is my heart.

—Frederick Peterson, American poet
(1859-1938)